The Changing Contours of
British Industrial Relations

A Survey of Manufacturing Industry

Warwick Studies in Industrial Relations

General Editors: G.S. Bain and H.A. Clegg

The Changing Contours of British Industrial Relations

A Survey of Manufacturing Industry

Edited by William Brown

With Contributions by
Eric Batstone · David Deaton
P.K. Edwards · Moira Hart
Keith Sisson · Brian Weekes

BASIL BLACKWELL · OXFORD

© Social Science Research Council 1981

First published in 1981 by
Basil Blackwell Publisher
108 Cowley Road
Oxford OX4 1JF
England

Reprinted 1982

British Library Cataloguing in Publication Data

The Changing contours of British industrial relations.
   1. Industrial relations — Great Britain
   I. Brown, William, 1945—
   331'.0941   HD8391

   ISBN 0-631-12775-5

Typeset by MHL Typesetting Ltd, Coventry
Printed in Great Britain by
The Blackwell Press, Guildford, London, Oxford, Worcester

Contents

List of Tables

Editors' Foreword

The University of Warwick is the major centre in the United Kingdom for the study of industrial relations. Its first undergraduates were admitted in 1965. The teaching of industrial relations began a year later in the School of Industrial and Business Studies, and it now has one of the country's largest graduate programmes in this subject. Warwick became a national centre for research into industrial relations in 1970 when the Social Science Research Council, a publicly funded body, located its Industrial Relations Research Unit at the University. The Unit has a full-time staff of about twenty and undertakes research into a wide range of topics in industrial relations.

The series of Warwick Studies in Industrial Relations was launched in 1972 as the main vehicle for the publication of the results of the Unit's projects. It is also intended to disseminate the research carried out by staff teaching industrial relations in the University, and the work of graduate students. The first six titles in the series were published by Heinemann Educational Books of London, and subsequent titles have been published by Basil Blackwell of Oxford.

The present monograph results from a survey of 970 manufacturing establishments. It was designed by the Unit and financed by the SSRC, with the fieldwork conducted by IFF Research Ltd. There were two objectives. The first was to obtain a more comprehensive 'map' of industrial relations in British manufacturing industry than previous surveys have given, by selecting a larger sample and asking a wider range of questions. The second was to seek answers to specific questions arising out of projects which were underway in the Unit at the time the survey was launched.

Some of the results have already appeared in articles, and others will do so in further articles and in monographs in this series. Here all the major results are brought together in a single volume which, by making comparisons with earlier surveys, provides a comprehensive analysis of the substantial changes that have occurred in many aspects of industrial relations in the 1970s.

G.S. Bain
H.A. Clegg

Preface

This study has been the outcome of team research from beginning to end. Staff of the Industrial Relations Research Unit and of the School of Industrial and Business Studies at Warwick University have collaborated in questionnaire design, data analysis, discussion of the results, and writing up. It was decided that this book should tell a 'story' and focus on a particular thread of argument rather than simply be a source book of statistical information. Consequently the role of the editor in bringing the various contributions into a coherent work has been a substantial one and it is only fair to the contributors to say that he should be held responsible for the emphases and final interpretations contained in the book. In addition to those mentioned on the title page, Linda Dickens, Michael Jones and Michael Terry were involved in data analysis and interpretation. Michael Terry also played a key role in liaison with the firm carrying out the survey. Olivia Amphlett was responsible for the computing and Connie Bussman for the secretarial sides of the project.

The research team is indebted to many people outside Warwick. First and foremost to Malcolm Rigg and his colleagues at IFF Research Ltd. whose conduct of the survey was exemplary. It was a rare pleasure to work with people so capable of combining efficiency with attentiveness to academic needs. In addition, Douglas Brooks, Bill Daniel, Bill McCarthy, Bob McKersie, and Stanley Parker gave helpful advice at various stages. Apart from paying most of the contributors' salaries, the Social Science Research Council earns their gratitude by the rapid and ready way in which it provided funds; in particular Derek Robinson, at that time Chairman, took a personal interest in the project that was much appreciated. Department of Employment staff kindly helped us to check strike statistics. Finally, warm thanks are due to the many hundreds of personnel and industrial relations managers who gave us their time and views. We hope that they will find this analysis of the results worthwhile.

1

Introduction

The most comprehensive survey of the state of British industrial relations was made by the Royal Commission under Lord Donovan between 1965 and 1968. The present study is based on a survey of manufacturing establishments carried out over the winter of 1977–78, almost ten years after Donovan reported. Its principal objective was to obtain a representative picture of the conduct of industrial relations in manufacturing industry, the sector of employment with which Donovan was primarily concerned, which would allow an assessment of the extent of change over the intervening decade. Besides enabling us to construct an institutional 'map', the survey was also designed to cast light on a wide range of theories and controversies.

It was essential that the survey's findings should be statistically representative. With very few exceptions (Commission on Industrial Relations, 1973; Daniel, 1976), previous surveys have relied on a degree of self-selection by respondents (Marsh *et al*., 1971; Brown *et al*., 1978) or have not been designed in such a way that the findings could be generalised to a whole population (Government Social Survey, 1968; Parker, 1974 and 1975). The present survey did not attempt to be representative of the whole of industry, being limited to manufacturing establishments with fifty or more employees. Sampling and definitional problems would have made it difficult to extend its coverage to non-manufacturing. In any event the greater variety, and often more rudimentary nature, of institutions outside manufacturing would have strained the questions. Similar considerations required the exclusion of small plants, but since those with fewer than fifty employees account for only 15 per cent of manufacturing employment our survey is representative of the experience of the great majority of employees in manufacturing.

The technical details of the survey and its representativeness are given in an appendix. The managers responsible for industrial relations

1

2

TABLE 1.1

WORKFORCE CHARACTERISTICS OF ESTABLISHMENTS BY INDUSTRY

	All Manufacturing	Food, Drink, Tobacco	Chemicals etc	Metal Manufacture	Mechanical Engineering and Ships	Instrument and Electrical Engineering	Vehicles	Metal Goods N.E.S	Textiles	Clothing, Leather, Footwear	Bricks, Timber and Misc.	Paper, Printing and Pub.
S.I.C. Category	3–19	3	4, 5	6	7, 10	8, 9	11	12	13	14, 15	16, 17, 19	18
Establishments in sample	970	110	74	76	107	113	67	95	66	78	97	87
Establishments in population	20397	1979	1051	1004	2971	1879	997	1856	1921	1903	3039	1797
Average workforce size	294	290	353	430	298	382	729	197	212	163	197	217
Components of average establishment workforce expressed as percentage of full-time employees — women	30.5	30	27	12	20	40	21	19	49	64	19	32
part-time employees	5.2	7	3	2	3	6	2	3	6	10	3	11
non-manual employees	27.8	22	39	25	35	33	29	27	22	21	21	37
managers	8.5	6	11	6	8	10	9	9	9	8	8	10

at 970 establishments were interviewed, the response rate was 68 per cent and there were no obvious sources of bias. The sample was stratified by industry and workforce size and, to maintain adequate sample sizes within industries, certain groups of the Standard Industrial Classification with similarities in collective bargaining arrangements were combined. We thus operate with eleven industrial groups; various characteristics of establishments in each group are given in Table 1.1.

The questions were largely confined to fairly straightforward matters of fact. More subjective questions on, for example, managers' impressions of their discretion in handling industrial relations problems should be approached with caution. Similar care should be used in interpreting perceptions of change. Where we make comparisons with previous surveys we indicate their statistical strength; where no such data are available we have to rely upon respondents' impressions. The map of practices and institutions that results is inevitably fairly crude and, being concerned with broad patterns and general tendencies, leaves room for many exceptions. It tells us little about the processes at work except in so far as they can be deduced from associations between variables. Any survey must be interpreted in conjunction with observation, case studies, and other empirical techniques. Many of the findings are presented in the form of simple statistical description, normally analysed by industry and size of establishment. They are, unless otherwise stated, weighted to be descriptive of the whole population sampled. Because the incidence of many phenomena varies with establishment size we have tried to control for this when testing for associations between variables, normally by breaking the sample into two or more size bands and seeing whether the relationship still holds within each. Where it has been necessary to control for more than one variable at a time we have used more complex multivariate techniques which are described briefly in the technical appendix. The fact that many hundreds of tests have been conducted in the course of the analysis presents a major problem of presentation: to spell them out would be tedious and impractical. Readers wanting further information may apply to the Unit or use the basic data in the SSRC Survey Archive at the University of Essex.

This survey and its analysis have been shaped by the interests of a team of researchers working on a variety of projects at the Industrial Relations Research Unit: projects on employers' associations, workplace bargaining, industrial democracy, third party intervention, industrial conflict, and labour hoarding. Some results have already been published in article form (Bain and Elsheikh, 1980; Deaton and Beaumont, 1980; Edwards, 1980 and forthcoming) and others will follow. Further use of the survey will be made in subsequent publications in this monograph series arising from individual projects.

The next chapter analyses the structure of pay bargaining in manufacturing industry and, finding that it has undergone substantial change, considers the consequences of this for employers' organisations. Chapter 3 looks at industrial relations management and its recent development, and also at the disputes procedures that the Donovan Commission was keen to encourage. Chapter 4 turns to trade union organisation at the workplace and finds the position of shop stewards to have changed substantially over the decade. Chapter 5 presents an analysis of the incidence of industrial action. Chapter 6 considers a number of aspects of personnel and employment policy. The final chapter draws together the main conclusions.

2

Bargaining Levels and Employers' Organisations

A central characteristic of industrial relations in any country where collective bargaining is relatively free from state control is the level at which pay is negotiated. Another way of looking at essentially the same question is to focus on the choice of bargaining units: the groups of employees covered by particular agreements. At various times and places in British industry almost every possible form of bargaining unit has been used. Sometimes the employers in an industry have formed an association, either on a regional or nationwide basis, in order to negotiate terms. At other times individual employers have gone their own way but have differed in the extent to which they have dealt uniformly or separately with all the establishments in their company. The most typical outcome of this varied historical development is a mixture of bargaining levels. Thus whether an item is fixed by an industry-wide agreement at one extreme, or by a workshop one at the other, varies both with the issue and with the group of employees in question.

This chapter attempts to bring some order to this complexity by concentrating on one issue, pay, and two broad categories of employee, manual and non-manual. An analysis of the levels of pay bargaining leads to a discussion of the role of the employers' associations. First, however, it is necessary to clarify some problems of measurement and definition.

Our survey asked, for manual and non-manual workers separately, about the last pay settlement made for any major group. Out of the small minority of plants for which this group did not comprise the whole of the manual or non-manual workforce we excluded replies that covered less than 50 per cent of the workforce. Our analysis is thus based upon the 96 per cent of establishments for which the replies are representative of at least half the manual workforce. The figure for non-manuals is 95 per cent.

The survey was conducted in late 1977 and early 1978 at a time of a national incomes policy. We asked under which stage of policy the last settlement had been made. For both manual and non-manual groups 55 per cent of establishments had settled under what was known as Phase Two which provided for a maximum increase of 5 per cent within the limits of £2.50 and £4 per week (Cmnd 6507). Almost all the remainder, 44 per cent, had settled under the looser constraints of the subsequent Phase: settlements had to be 'well within single figures' for establishments as a whole but exception was made for the introduction of occupational pension schemes and self-financing productivity deals (Cmnd 6882). The remaining one per cent had not settled their pay since Phase One's £6 limit (Cmnd 6151). The self-financing productivity deal option of Phase Two had been used in 43 per cent of establishments, with a further 14 per cent contemplating it; use of the option was greater among large than among small establishments. Some consequences of the survey coinciding with an incomes policy will be returned to.

A list of possible institutional arrangements for pay fixing was presented to respondents and they were asked 'at which of the following levels were negotiations or discussions conducted which affected this settlement?' For the minority mentioning more than one level (14 per cent for manuals and 5 per cent for non-manuals) we asked 'and which would you say was the most important?' with the amplifying prompt of 'gave rise to the largest part of increase'.

The first level listed was 'negotiations through a statutory wages board or council'. Second was 'industry-wide agreements involving more than one employer', followed by 'regional or district negotiations involving several local employers'. We have combined as 'corporate' the next two categories of negotiation — 'at your group or total organisation level also covering similar workers elsewhere in the organisation', and 'at divisional level of your organisation or group' because it was apparent that respondents interpreted the distinction differently. Next we specified 'negotiations or discussions covering only workers employed here at this establishment'. The final two categories were for 'other negotiations or discussions', and for 'no negotiations or discussions between employers and workers or their representatives'.

The responses revealed that employers in industries where there had once been wages councils often confused these with the national joint industrial councils that had taken their place. We have thus grouped together the first two categories of reply as 'industry-wide'.

The Level of Manual Pay Bargaining

Collective bargaining is of overwhelming importance in manual workers' pay determination in manufacturing. As Table 2.1 shows, only 10 per cent of establishments (with at least 50 employees) employing 4 per cent of the workforce reported that no negotiations or discussions took place over pay. These are, as Table 2.2 shows, mostly the smaller establishments, there being no negotiations in 17 per cent of places with between 50 and 99 employees. Even when this size effect is allowed for, an absence of negotiations is significantly more common in single-plant as opposed to multi-plant establishments.

Among those establishments where negotiations had occurred, an initial question is the extent to which they took place at more than one level for individual establishments. Daniel's pioneering survey of 1975 showed bargaining at more than one level to be commonplace (1976; 26). Our results on this matter are probably influenced by the form of incomes policy prevailing at the time of our survey. The simplicity of the policy rules undoubtedly reduced the likelihood of employees' being affected by more than one set of negotiations. Thus, while Daniel had found, during a period of relatively free collective bargaining, that 39 per cent of his establishments reported bargaining at two levels and 13 per cent at three or more, our results were very different. Taking unweighted results for the purpose of comparison, our comparable figures were 14 per cent with two levels and 3 per cent with three or more. It made no difference whether the last settlement had been under Phase Two or Phase Three but bargaining at more than one level was slightly more common where firms had concluded self-financing productivity deals under Phase Three. It is likely that a relaxation of incomes policy would lead to an increase in multi-level bargaining.

Our survey is more instructive when we turn from the number of levels of settlement to the level considered most important which for the great majority, as has just been noted, had been the only level. The proportion of establishments and of employees covered by the different levels of bargaining appears in the first column of Table 2.1 Multi-employer agreements cover 27 per cent of manual workers. Within the multi-employer arrangements, industry-wide agreements (including wages council awards) are most important for 33 per cent of establishments (24 per cent of employees) and regional agreements for 3 per cent of both establishments and employees. For the single-employer agreements, those at corporate level cover 11 per cent of establishments but 21 per cent of employees, while those covering single establishments were effective at 42 per cent with 46 per cent of employees.

TABLE 2.1

THE LEVEL OF BARGAINING MOST IMPORTANT FOR MANUAL WAGES BY INDUSTRY PERCENTAGE OF ESTABLISHMENTS

(Percentage of establishments; percentage of employees in parentheses; percentages less than 0.6 indicated by –)

Level of Agreement	All Manufacturing	Food, Drink, Tobacco	Chemicals etc.	Metal Manufacturing	Mechanical Engineering and Ships	Instrument and Electrical Engineering	Vehicles	Metal Goods N.E.S.	Textiles	Clothing Footwear etc.	Bricks, Timber, and Misc.	Paper, Printing and Publishing
Industry-wide	33.2 (24.0)	50 (33)	25 (19)	6 (11)	8 (8)	2 (4)	10 (3)	7 (6)	67 (54)	72 (58)	42 (35)	66 (82)
Regional	3.0 (2.7)	1 (1)	– (1)	11 (4)	2 (1)	– (–)	5 (3)	3 (4)	6 (7)	3 (5)	3 (4)	3 (2)
All multi-employer	36.2 (26.7)	51 (34)	25 (20)	17 (15)	10 (9)	2 (4)	15 (6)	10 (10)	73 (61)	75 (63)	45 (39)	69 (84)
Corporate	11.3 (21.1)	17 (32)	20 (24)	19 (35)	9 (17)	3 (15)	12 (36)	15 (18)	3 (8)	11 (20)	16 (16)	4 (1)
Establishment	41.6 (46.5)	19 (25)	41 (50)	60 (48)	71 (71)	60 (67)	72 (56)	60 (65)	21 (27)	12 (12)	31 (39)	16 (13)
All single-employer	52.9 (67.6)	36 (57)	61 (74)	79 (83)	80 (88)	63 (82)	84 (90)	75 (83)	24 (35)	23 (32)	47 (55)	20 (14)
Other	1.2 (1.3)	5 (2)	6 (4)	– (–)	– (–)	2 (1)	1 (3)	– (1)	1 (1)	– (–)	– (1)	– (2)
No bargaining	9.8 (4.4)	8 (7)	6 (3)	4 (2)	10 (4)	34 (13)	– (–)	13 (5)	3 (3)	2 (5)	9 (5)	9 (1)
TOTAL	100.0 (100.0)	100 (100)	100 (100)	100 (100)	100 (100)	100 (100)	100 (100)	100 (100)	100 (100)	100 (100)	100 (100)	100 (100)

TABLE 2.2

THE LEVEL OF BARGAINING MOST IMPORTANT FOR MANUAL WAGES BY SIZE OF ESTABLISHMENT

(Percentage of establishments; percentage of employees in parentheses)

Level of Agreement	Size of Establishment by Number of Full-Time Employees				
	50–99	100–199	200–499	500–999	1000+
Industry-wide	43 (46)	28 (28)	28 (30)	21 (23)	14 (11)
Regional	1 (1)	5 (5)	4 (5)	2 (2)	1 (–)
All multi-employer	44 (47)	33 (33)	32 (35)	23 (25)	15 (11)
Corporate	7 (8)	11 (12)	15 (14)	16 (18)	32 (38)
Establishment	32 (32)	48 (47)	45 (45)	54 (52)	52 (49)
All single-employer	39 (40)	59 (59)	60 (59)	70 (70)	84 (87)
Other	– (–)	2 (2)	1 (1)	2 (2)	1 (1)
No bargaining	17 (13)	5 (6)	6 (5)	4 (3)	– (–)
TOTAL	100 (100)	100 (100)	100 (100)	100 (100)	100 (100)

The only previous study to have looked at this question is Daniel's 1975 survey (1976; 28). To make our results comparable with his we have had to use unweighted (probability proportional to workforce size) data on establishments with more than 200 employees where unions were recognised. Bearing in mind that the earlier study related to bargaining far less constrained by incomes policy than our own, Daniel found that 17 per cent of his establishments reported that the 'national' level was the most important compared with 24 per cent of ours which were covered by either industry-wide or wages council arrangements. Two per cent of his respondents reported regional or district agreements compared with three per cent of ours. Company or divisional levels were most important for 20 per cent of Daniel's compared with 21 per cent of ours. The establishment was named by 55 per cent of respondents in the earlier survey compared with 48 per cent of a comparable extract of ours. There is, therefore, considerable consistency with Daniel's findings when we take into account the fact that our survey coincided with an incomes policy which is likely to have made many employers revert to multi-employer arrangements. Under free collective bargaining individual employers are more likely to act alone. The results analysed here are thus likely to present a cautious picture of the extent of single employer bargaining.

As Table 2.1 shows, the divide between single- and multi-employer arrangements for manual workers' pay varies substantially between industries. The picture can be characterised in broad terms. The five metal-working industry groups are similar in their reliance upon single-employer bargaining for both small and large workforces. Close behind them are the chemicals and associated industries, perhaps partly because, as Table 1.1 shows, they also have above average workforce size. Multi-employer agreements continue to be important for the smaller chemicals plants, but for three-quarters of the employees in the industry it is the single-employer arrangements that matter most.

At the other extreme, paper and printing stand out as industries where, for all workforce sizes, the multi-employer agreement has preserved its strength. Single-employer bargaining here is particularly unusual among the larger workforces. Another group of industries where multi-employer arrangements still dominate is textiles, clothing, footwear, leather, and fur; single-employer bargaining applies to only a third of their workforces. The catch-all bricks, pottery, glass, cement, timber, furniture, and miscellaneous category, and that of food, drink and tobacco, rely on multi-employer arrangements for approximately half of their establishments but for a substantially smaller part of their total employment — over half of their employees are covered by single-employer arrangements.

The size of the workforce has a strong association with the level of pay agreement used. From Table 2.2 it can be seen that, overall, multi-employer bargaining diminishes in importance according to the size of the workforce: multi-employer arrangements are most important for 47 per cent of the workforce in establishments of between 50 and 99 employees but for only 11 per cent in those of more than a thousand.

Foreign ownership also appears to have an influence upon the choice of bargaining level. Not only did 15 per cent of foreign-owned establishments have no pay bargaining compared with 9 per cent of British establishments; there were 63 per cent of foreign-owned establishments with single-employer agreements compared with 50 per cent of British.

Taking each size-band in turn, there is strong evidence that foreign-owned companies tend to avoid multi-employer pay fixing arrangements for their manual workers and prefer independence. This is consistent with the study of foreign-owned subsidiaries by Gennard and Steuer (1971). Foreign ownership of British manufacturing, the bulk of which is American, may have been an important stimulant to the decay of multi-employer bargaining.

The increase in incidence of single-employer bargaining arrangements with establishment size comes less from the contribution of establishment than of corporate agreements. It will be recalled that the term 'corporate' is being used to refer to agreements which cover more than one, but not necessarily all, establishments in a multi-establishment firm. This rising importance of corporate agreements with an establishment's workforce size deserves further consideration. As will be shown in the next chapter, there is a strong tendency in British manufacturing for larger establishments to be part of multi-plant enterprises. Thus the opportunity to have a corporate agreement increases with establishment size. Establishments that are part of multi-plant enterprises are no more likely to have single-employer bargaining than are single establishments of comparable size. It is only for the smallest (50 to 99 employees) band that the incidence of single-employer bargaining is markedly greater for multi-plant than single-plant establishments. However, the propensity of multi-plant establishments to be covered by corporate as opposed to establishment agreements does increase with workforce size.

Thus workforce size appears to be a factor influencing the decision of multi-plant companies to have corporate, as opposed to establishment, single-employer bargaining. Foreign ownership also appears to be an influence: 16 per cent of foreign-owned establishments had corporate agreements compared with 10 per cent of British. Looking at the practice of different industries, Table 2.1 shows that in the four engineering industry categories establishment level bargaining is dominant, although corporate agreements are important among the larger vehicle factories. In chemicals and metal manufacturing a substantial proportion of establishments are covered by corporate agreements. Among the rest, food, drink and tobacco, clothing, footwear, etc., and the bricks, timber and miscellaneous industrial categories are distinctive in that a relatively high proportion of such single-employer arrangements as they have take a corporate form. The evidence on bargaining reforms presented in subsequent chapters suggests that many companies in this last group, which is generally characterised by little tradition of workplace bargaining, have moved straight to corporate bargaining from multi-employer arrangements without any intermediate phase at establishment level.

TABLE 2.3

THE LEVEL OF BARGAINING MOST IMPORTANT FOR NON-MANUAL WAGES BY INDUSTRY

(Percentage of establishments; percentage of employees in parentheses)

Level of Agreement	All Manufacturing	Food, Drink, Tobacco	Chemicals etc.	Metal Manufacturing	Mechanical Engineering and Ships	Instrument and Electrical Engineering	Vehicles	Metal Goods N.E.S.	Textiles	Clothing Footwear etc.	Bricks, Timber and Misc.	Paper, Printing and Publishing
Industry-wide	17.2 (8.3)	47 (21)	– (–)	1 (1)	5 (4)	1 (–)	9 (1)	2 (3)	20 (21)	42 (28)	20 (10)	33 (38)
Regional	1.3 (0.9)	– (–)	– (–)	4 (1)	– (–)	– (–)	– (–)	2 (1)	5 (5)	2 (4)	– (1)	– (2)
All multi-employer	18.5 (9.2)	47 (21)	– (–)	5 (2)	5 (4)	1 (–)	9 (1)	4 (4)	25 (26)	44 (32)	20 (11)	33 (40)
Corporate	14.9 (28.6)	26 (34)	23 (33)	25 (47)	11 (20)	8 (29)	16 (49)	17 (22)	11 (18)	12 (10)	19 (26)	5 (9)
Establishment	39.5 (44.7)	13 (25)	28 (38)	45 (40)	65 (64)	54 (54)	48 (42)	52 (56)	15 (29)	25 (40)	39 (41)	37 (23)
All single-employer	54.4 (73.3)	39 (59)	51 (71)	70 (87)	76 (84)	62 (83)	64 (91)	69 (78)	26 (47)	37 (50)	58 (67)	42 (32)
Other	2.0 (2.8)	2 (6)	7 (6)	5 (–)	1 (3)	1 (3)	4 (3)	– (–)	– (–)	– (1)	4 (3)	2 (3)
No bargaining	25.1 (14.7)	12 (15)	42 (22)	19 (10)	18 (10)	36 (14)	23 (6)	26 (18)	49 (26)	18 (16)	18 (20)	23 (25)
TOTAL	100.0 (100.0)	100 (100)	100 (100)	100 (100)	100 (100)	100 (100)	100 (100)	100 (100)	100 (100)	100 (100)	100 (100)	100 (100)

In a study using the statistical technique of discriminant analysis on these data, Deaton and Beaumont have explored the choice of multi-employer as opposed to single-employer bargaining, taking eleven variables as possible determinants and controlling between them (Deaton and Beaumont, 1980). They found that 'high regional concentration, high union density, and multi-unionism are associated with multi-employer bargaining, whereas larger establishments, multi-plant firms, foreign owner firms, high concentration industries and firms with [specialist] industrial relations management tend to have single-employer bargaining.' They were not, however, able to distinguish any clear features besides establishment size that might cast light on the choice between establishment and corporate bargaining. Nor is this surprising, for this choice is strongly affected by the heterogeneity of a company's products and by the history of its evolution by merger, take-over, or internal growth.

Our question about the phase of incomes policy under which the respondents' establishments had last settled pay produced a finding that has an important bearing upon the significance to be attached to different bargaining levels. Multi-employer bargainers were very much less likely to have settled under the new pay round than single-employer bargainers. With the Phase Three policy some four months old, only 29 per cent of those covered by multi-employer arrangements reported settling under it. But as many as 55 per cent of the single-employer bargainers had already settled under Phase Three: 49 per cent of corporate and 57 per cent of establishment agreements. This is strong evidence that single-employer bargainers (and especially establishment-level bargainers) take the lead in wage bargaining, with the multi-employer bargains following in their wake. It supports the view that single-employer bargaining has particular causal significance in manufacturing wage determination (Brown and Terry, 1978).

The Level of Non-Manual Pay Bargaining

There have been no previous studies of the level at which the pay of non-manual workers is fixed in manufacturing. It is with some surprise that we note how extensive pay bargaining has become. As can be seen from the first column of Table 2.3, although no bargaining takes place on non-manual pay at 25 per cent of establishments with 50 or more employees, these cover only 15 per cent of the non-manual workforce. As Table 2.4 shows, an absence of bargaining is closely related to establishment size; there is no bargaining in 32 per cent of plants in the 50 to 99 total employment category but in only 8 per cent of those with a thousand or more employees.

TABLE 2.4

THE LEVEL OF BARGAINING MOST IMPORTANT FOR NON-MANUAL WAGES BY SIZE OF ESTABLISHMENT

(Percentage of establishments; percentage of employees in parentheses)

Level of Agreement	Size of Establishment by Number of Full-Time Employees				
	50−99	100−199	200−499	500−999	1000+
Industry-wide	23 (23)	15 (10)	13 (11)	8 (7)	4 (4)
Regional	− (−)	3 (2)	2 (1)	1 (1)	− (−)
All multi-employer	23 (23)	18 (12)	15 (12)	9 (8)	4 (4)
Corporate	7 (6)	16 (13)	23 (20)	22 (20)	39 (48)
Establishment	36 (43)	40 (47)	41 (45)	50 (55)	46 (39)
All single-employer	43 (49)	56 (60)	64 (65)	72 (75)	85 (87)
Other	2 (1)	1 (2)	3 (4)	3 (3)	2 (2)
No bargaining	32 (28)	25 (27)	18 (18)	15 (13)	8 (6)
TOTAL	100 (100)	100 (100)	100 (100)	100 (100)	100 (100)

For non-manual workers, single-employer arrangements are overwhelmingly more important than those of multi-employer organisations. Multi-employer agreements cover 18 per cent of establishments but only 9 per cent of employees.

Among the single-employer arrangements the importance of establishment agreements is much the same as for manuals: they apply at 39 per cent of establishments and cover 45 per cent of non-manual employees. But corporate agreements are of greater importance for non-manual than for manual employees: they cover 15 per cent of establishments employing 29 per cent of non-manual employees. Thus, non-manual pay bargaining in manufacturing essentially means single-employer pay bargaining, covering 73 per cent of non-manual workers at 54 per cent of establishments with over 50 employees. Only 5 per cent reported that non-manual bargaining had occurred at more than one bargaining level.

Here again, establishment size appears to play an important part. As Table 2.4 shows, the larger the workforce one looks at the more likely it is to have a single-employer agreement for non-manual workers — the more likely also that it will be a corporate agreement. Almost half the non-manual employees in establishments of a thousand or more workers are covered by corporate agreements. It is a feature to which white collar unions have, as we shall see, responded more readily than their manual counterparts by the formation of combine committees of shop stewards.

As with manual bargaining, single-employer agreements were more common for non-manual workers in multi-plant establishments and this was largely accounted for by their greater size. There was a clear tendency for multi-plant establishments to make greater use of corporate agreements the greater their workforce size. Foreign-owned enterprises do not differ from the British ones in their use of single-employer agreements for non-manual workers. There are some clear signs that foreign-owned firms are more opposed than British ones to negotiating with their non-manual workers (or that they find less need to do so): 34 per cent of foreign establishments have no non-manual bargaining compared with 23 per cent of British, and this difference applies across all size bands.

Multi-employer agreements are rare for non-manual workers in the chemicals and engineering industries. Industry-wide agreements are fairly important in clothing and footwear and in food, drink and tobacco. But even in paper and printing, where industry-wide agreements have the greatest extent in terms of employees, they cover only a little over a third of the workforce. For the rest, the emphasis upon establishment agreements is moderated by corporate arrangements that are particularly important in the food, chemicals, metal manufacture, and bricks and miscellaneous groups.

To answer the question of why enterprises choose to bargain with their non-manual workers at the level they do, the best clue comes from Table 2.5. This shows the degree of correspondence between manual and non-manual bargaining arrangements. For each level of manual bargaining the table indicates the breakdown of arrangements used for non-manuals at the establishments concerned, the rows adding up to 100 per cent. It is immediately evident from the strong diagonal line that the correspondence between the two negotiations is high. Where multi-employer arrangements are used for manuals they are matched by similar arrangements for non-manuals in a minority of cases and either an absence of any bargaining or single bargaining arrangements cover the remainder. But where single bargaining agreements are used for manuals then in the great majority of cases the same level of agreement is used for the non-manuals as well. It is likely that where an employer adopts an independent policy for his manuals he generally integrates his non-manual policy with it.

TABLE 2.5

CORRESPONDENCE BETWEEN MANUAL AND NON-MANUAL LEVELS OF BARGAINING

Level of Agreement for *Manual* Workers	Percentage of Establishments for which the Level of Agreement for *Non-Manuals* is:					
	Industry-wide	Regional	Corporate	Establishment	Other	None
Industry-wide	45	–	12	23	5	15
Regional	13	38	1	12	8	28
Corporate	–	–	83	4	–	12
Establishment	2	–	8	75	1	13
Other	–	7	–	48	43	2
None	7	–	1	1	–	92

The Operation of Industry-Wide Agreements

In 1968 the Donovan Commission noted that a 'remarkable transfer of authority in collective bargaining' had occurred over the previous thirty years with the declining influence of industry-wide agreements over pay. But the Commissioners declared themselves unable to say just how effective these agreements remained (Royal Commission, 1968: 14, 37). In the following years some of the most important employers' associations responded to the declining effectiveness of the agreements by altering them in such a way that they provided only minimum rates of pay whose alteration would not necessarily affect the earnings of workers covered by the agreement but earning above the minima. The very large engineering and chemicals agreements were altered in this way as well as smaller ones such as those for hosiery and rubber (C.I.R., 1972: 21).

A recent study has characterised this shift in the nature of industry-wide agreements as one from providing a 'floor' whose rates raise all earnings when they are raised, to merely providing a 'safety net' whereby only the earnings of the relatively low paid are affected. 'At a conservative estimate, multi-employer agreements are probably providing no more than "safety net" support for the wages of two thirds of all manual employees in manufacturing' (Brown and Terry, 1978: 125). The present survey sharpens this estimate with the finding that only 27 per cent of manual employees in manufacturing have multi-employer agreements as their most important source of wage increases.

Despite this decline in the significance of industry-wide agreements, membership of employers' associations, as we discuss later, shows no sign of substantial decline. Furthermore, when we asked whether establishments followed industry-wide agreements for their manual employees, the replies indicated that 70 per cent of establishments (covering 73 per cent of employees) did so. Since, however, our definition of 'following' included both partial and indirect adherence, an affirmative reply could have indicated that the employer used the agreement for no more than the size of shift premia or the length of the basic week.

It was informative to see which establishments followed industry-wide agreements. Establishments of over 1,000 employees and those of under 200 employees were less likely to do so than average. Over a third of those indicating that they followed an agreement said it was the one for manual workers in the engineering industry which, since 1971, has provided only 'safety net' minima. There is little congruence between being a member of an employers' association and following a multi-employer agreement. As many as 51 per cent of establishments which were not employers' association members said that they followed industry-wide agreements; conversely, the two industries with the lowest proportion of establishments following an industry-wide agreement, textiles and chemicals, were among those with the highest proportion in membership of employers' associations.

We failed in a further attempt to explore how industry-wide agreements influence wages. Thomson, Mulvey, and Farbman had made an attempt at the question using data from the 1973 New Earnings Survey (1977: 178). But the definition used by the N.E.S. failed to draw any distinction between single- and multi-employer agreements and the results are difficult to interpret. We therefore asked questions (given in the Appendix) designed to elicit whether agreements provided, among other things, for 'floors' or 'safety nets' to wages. But there were problems in asking hypothetical questions about what would occur in the absence of incomes policy and the replies were unusable. It was not only that they were wildly inconsistent with the replies to questions about bargaining levels; they also revealed widespread ignorance about the nature of the agreement that was purportedly being followed.

Our failure is probably indicative of the irrelevance for most enter-

TABLE 2.6

MEMBERSHIP OF EMPLOYERS' ORGANISATIONS AND OF CONFEDERATION OF BRITISH INDUSTRY BY INDUSTRY

(As a percentage of all establishments)

	per cent of all Employees	per cent of all Establishments	Food, Drink, Tobacco	Chemicals etc.	Metal Manufacturing	Mechanical Engineering and Ships	Instrument and Electrical Engineering	Vehicles	Metal Goods N.E.S.	Textiles	Clothing Footwear etc.	Bricks, Timber and Misc.	Paper, Printing and Publishing
Member of Employers' Organisation	72.2	75.0	78	74	75	71	71	77	79	82	70	74	76
Affiliation to the CBI { direct	38.5	29.0	23	34	30	26	32	37	35	21	24	33	31
indirect	39.8	45.3	27	50	52	44	35	44	50	66	41	46	46

prises of industry-wide agreements; employers are out of touch with their provisions. The same finding emerged when the 1968 New Earnings Survey asked employers to give industry-wide wage rate data appropriate to their employees. The employers who could do so tended only to be those paying close to those rates (Brown and Terry, 1978: 121). Ten years later the multi-employer industry-wide agreement has been still further eclipsed.

Employers' Associations

Although the importance of their industry-wide pay agreements has been declining in recent years, employers' associations remain prominent industrial relations institutions. We were concerned to find out the extent of their membership and the nature of their work. Previous studies have tended to rely upon information supplied by the employers' associations themselves (McCarthy, 1967: Commission of Industrial Relations, 1972); we were able to ask questions at establishment level.

Seventy-five per cent of establishments replied that they were members of an employers' organisation. They covered 72 per cent of employees. It is likely that some of these organisations were not employers' associations in the strict sense, and the fact that managers perceive trade associations and the like as having relevance to employment issues is itself of interest. There was no systematic variation in membership with establishment size, nor did it seem to make much difference whether or not they were part of multi-plant companies. Foreign ownership appears to have some effect in inhibiting membership, but it is only slight; 69 per cent of foreign-owned establishments being in employers' organisations compared with 75 per cent of British.

This even pattern continues when we look at the distribution of employer association membership by industry. Table 2.6 shows it to be nowhere less than 70 per cent. There was, however, considerable complexity in the number of associations. The 40 large ones that we named in the questionnaire covered only 58 per cent of establishments. The only organisations that had more than half the establishments in any one industrial order in membership were the Engineering Employers' Federation, the British Printing Industries Federation, the British Textile Employers' Association, and the Chemical Industries Association. Most complex was the food, drink and tobacco group of industries, where the 9 organisations we named covered only half the total membership of employers' associations in the group. As already noted, it is likely that some of our respondents were referring to trade associations rather than employers' associations and these results should be treated with caution.

To find out how this picture was changing, we asked non-members whether they had ever been in an employers' association and, if so, how long it had been since they had left. Four per cent said that they had once been in membership and they tended to be among the larger establishments. They were disproportionately evident in metal manufacture, instrument and electrical engineering, and paper and printing. Over a third of them had left their associations a decade or more ago. In short, there are no signs that there has been either a sudden or a mass exodus from employers' associations.

Besides negotiating some form of industry-wide agreement on terms and conditions of employment, a second function of most employers' associations is often one of operating a procedure for the resolution of disputes that might arise between member firms and trade unions. Association members are more likely than non-members to recognise trade unions: 80 per cent of members recognised one or more trade unions compared with 67 per cent of non-members. Although 65 per cent of all establishments which were members said that their association operated a disputes procedure, many respondents seemed poorly informed. A substantial proportion of E.E.F. and C.I.A. members, for instance, denied the existence of their association's procedure.

Almost half of the establishments which said that their association provided an external procedure had made use of it in the previous two years. On average, members had used external procedures just over twice during the period with use being particularly heavy in engineering and printing. Larger establishments made considerably more use of external procedures than small ones: 75 per cent with 1,000 or more employees had done so compared with only 33 per cent with between 50 and 99 employees.

Usage of these external disputes procedures has tended to increase. Compared with five years previously 24 per cent of establishments which had procedures available to them were now using them more, and only 8 per cent were using them less. Of the major procedures, only that operated by the E.E.F. had a substantial proportion of firms reporting reduced usage and, in net terms, 19 per cent reported greater use of it. Printing industry procedures have seen a particularly marked rise in use. It has generally been the larger establishments that have reported a decline in their use of these external procedures. This probably reflects both increasing industrial relations activity at smaller establishments and the development of better internal procedures at the larger ones.

The most important role of British employers' associations may now lie in their provision of advisory services. We asked respondents which of a range of advisory and information services their association provided. Only 8 per cent of member establishments said that none were available. The service most commonly reported to be available was advice or assistance on labour law, which might range from information leaflets to representation at tribunals; 79 per cent of members reported the availability of legal assistance. Seventy per cent said that they could get advice on incomes policy questions and the same percentage said that they could get data on local pay levels. Information on education and training and advice on redundancy questions were both available to 61 per cent of members. Advice on work study and bonus schemes, on job evaluation, and information on recruitment were available to, respectively, 45, 43, and 41 per cent of members.

The proof of the service is in its usage, and we asked which of these services members had used during the previous two years. The replies are analysed in Table 2.7. Assistance with labour law matters was the most popular, with 57 per cent of members having drawn on it. Fifty per cent had used their associations' information on local pay levels, a useful confirmation of the importance of employers' pay surveys to the process of wage determination (Pay Board, 1974: 23; Brown and Sisson, 1975). Next most used was association advice on the interpretation of incomes policies: 45 per cent reported their use of this service. The two years' experience to which the question referred had been ones of the Social Contract policy for which the rules had been relatively straightforward but the supporting sanctions from the government were more obscure. Advice and materials on education and training were used by 27 per cent and on redundancy questions by 23 per cent of members. Finally, just under 10 per cent of members sought help on questions of recruitment and payment systems.

The overall picture is one of establishments using their employers' associations primarily on questions where the government and its legislation are important. In addition they are widely used for pay bargaining data. The emphasis varies between industries. For instance there is relatively low utilisation of the services that the C.I.A. is reported to provide and it is the smaller associations whose general management services are most used. But one theory that can be dismissed is that employers' associations are primarily used by the smaller establishment which might lack specialist resources. As can be seen by the analysis by workforce size in Table 2.7, most services have greater utilisation by large than by small establishments. Furthermore, where there is an industrial relations specialist at a senior level in an establishment's management, use of the association is greater than where there is none. On some matters, such as where legal questions on employee rights are

TABLE 2.7

THE UTILISATION OF EMPLOYERS' ASSOCIATION ADVISORY SERVICES BY INDUSTRY AND SIZE

(As a percentage of establishments in association membership)

	Recruitment Information	Education and Training	Labour Legislation	Work Study or Bonus Schemes	Job Evaluation	Redundancy Policy	Local Pay Levels	Incomes Policy
Engineering Employers' Fed.	6	35	76	8	11	32	62	59
Other Engineering	2	41	51	28	16	47	30	41
Chemical Industries Assn.	5	11	31	17	8	46	28	29
Any Food etc.	1	16	37	9	10	24	33	33
Any Textiles	21	26	79	10	10	14	82	72
Any Clothing	12	45	65	48	36	43	52	52
Any Paper/Printing	24	45	72	32	23	36	62	64
Any Other	6	19	49	2	3	6	45	36
Number of 50–99	4	15	51	5	5	19	47	38
Full-time 100–199	16	31	58	16	12	26	48	43
Employees 200–499	9	37	61	11	11	22	56	52
500–999	7	49	72	13	15	17	54	59
1000+	14	42	75	13	15	24	62	68
ALL	9.0	27.1	57.4	9.9	9.2	21.6	50.4	44.8

concerned, one might expect their size to make for greater utilisation by the larger establishments, but this is less obviously the case when it comes to advice on incomes policy and local pay levels. Employers' associations appear to offer far more than just a poor man's industrial relations service.

This picture is reinforced when we consider the replies to the question of whether use of association services had increased or decreased in the past few years. Thirty-seven per cent of establishments reported an increase compared with only 2 per cent reporting a decrease. The net increase is substantially greater than that reported for the use of external dispute procedures and it occurs across industries, most notably for engineering and clothing. Establishments that reported that their own industrial relations function had increased in importance in recent years were particularly likely to say that their use of their employers' association had increased also.

Membership of the C.B.I.

These conclusions suggest that a major function of employers' associations has become one of helping individual firms in their dealings with the consequences of governmental action. For the Confederation of British Industry, governmental action has been the central focus of concern since its creation in 1965. Other studies have considered the C.B.I.'s membership in terms of the number of firms and associations covered; our survey gave us a first opportunity to assess its coverage in manufacturing industry in terms of establishments and employee numbers (Grant and Marsh, 1977).

We asked respondents whether their company affiliated directly to the C.B.I., or indirectly through a national or local employers' organisation. Overall, 74 per cent of establishments employing 78 per cent of the manufacturing workforce (4.2 million employees) are affiliated. Of these, 29 per cent of establishments (with 38 per cent of the workforce) have direct affiliation. There is a relatively high, 6 per cent, proportion of 'don't knows' and it is likely that the figures for indirect association are significantly understated since some members of the E.E.F. appeared to be unaware that this gives them indirect affiliation to the C.B.I.

The industrial breakdown of C.B.I. membership by establishment numbers is given in Table 2.6. It is highest in textiles and lowest in food. The larger an establishment's workforce, the more likely it was to be affiliated and the more likely it was to be affiliated directly. Whereas 69 per cent of establishments with between 50 and 99 employees were affiliated to the C.B.I., 19 per cent of them directly, 88 per cent of establishments with 1,000 or more employees were affiliated, 47 per cent directly. Non-members had an above average tendency to be single plant, foreign-owned, not members of the other employers' associations and not to recognise trade unions.

Conclusion

The most striking finding of this chapter has been that of the rise in significance of single-employer bargaining for manual workers. A decade earlier the Donovan Commission had described multi-employer negotiations involving employers' associations as the 'formal system' of industrial relations in manufacturing. This no longer holds. Single-employer bargaining has become the most important means of pay determination for two-thirds of manual workers. Among non-manual workers, for whom the significance of multi-employer bargaining had never been anything like as great, single-employer arrangements now determine pay for almost three-quarters of employees.

Although this shift to single-employer arrangements has been in accord with the prescriptions of the Donovan Commission, it would be unwise to ascribe it to any very conscious strategy on the part of employers. As the following chapters will demonstrate, managements have carried out a variety of reforms to workplace industrial relations. Changes have occurred in management's own organisation, in its relations with shop stewards, in procedures and in payment systems, many of them in response to the consequences of government actions. These changes have been difficult to reconcile with agreements covering large numbers of employers. But there has been no mass exodus from employers' associations. Instead employers have used their associations more as advisers than negotiators and have increasingly looked after negotiations for themselves. Consequently the move to single-employer bargaining is better seen as the largely unplanned consequence of piecemeal reform than as the deliberate rejection of established multi-employer arrangements.

The importance of this change should not be allowed to conceal the fact that for over a quarter of the manual workforce in manufacturing multi-employer pay bargaining continues to be of primary importance. There is an interesting parallel with the United States in the way in which industries with relatively low capital requirements and high ease of entry, such as printing and clothing, continue to rely heavily on multi-employer arrangements. Nor is there any reason to suppose that these will wither away. British manufacturing industry is likely to have a mixture of single- and multi-employer bargaining for the foreseeable future.

3

Industrial Relations Management and Disputes Procedures

Central to the proposals of the Donovan Commission was the reform of procedures, and the burden of carrying this out was placed upon management. From the board of directors downwards, management was urged to give greater priority to industrial relations matters than hitherto. Multi-employer bargaining, it was felt, 'fails to recognise the prime responsibility of boards of directors for industrial relations throughout their companies, and it thwarts attempts to design company personnel policies.' (Royal Commission, 1968: 44–5). The move to single-employer bargaining has been discussed at some length. In this chapter we describe where it has placed industrial relations management and what the consequences have been for the development of procedures.

The first concern is with the degree of specialisation of industrial relations management and how it has altered. Since most establishments are parts of larger enterprises the question arises as to how far management at establishment level has discretion to take its own decisions. It is one thing to have specialist managers but quite another to have their advice and policies heeded: how far respondents think this happens is the subject of the next section. After that, to place matters in a broader perspective, we enquire how important industrial relations considerations appear to be alongside the many other aspects of management when the general policy of an organisation is being formulated. The chapter ends with a survey of the extent and nature of disputes procedures.

The Specialisation of Industrial Relations Management

We enquired about specialist industrial relations management in two ways. First we asked our respondent, who had been selected at each establishment on the basis of being the manager most directly concerned with industrial relations matters, whether personnel and/or industrial relations were his main area of responsibility. It would have been possible to ask about, say, the number of staff for whom these subjects were a full-time concern, but the replies would have indicated nothing about their managerial seniority. Using our fairly restricted definition only 46 per cent of establishments had specialist respondents and, as Table 3.1 shows, their occurrence increased strongly with establishment size. Even with labour forces of 500 and more there was a significant proportion of places where the manager most responsible for industrial relations did not have it as his main responsibility.

The second, and less ambiguous, approach was to ask whether there was a director or someone at the highest level of the organisation whose specific responsibility was personnel and/or industrial relations, and then to ask whether it was his *sole* responsibility. Two-thirds of establishments (67 per cent) reported a director with this responsibility, and for 30 per cent it was his sole one. Table 3.1 gives the incidence by workforce size and demonstrates that even the largest establishments may have no director with specific responsibility for industrial relations matters.

Do firms develop specialist industrial relations management roles in response to bargaining pressures, or are there broader aspects or organisations of which this specialisation is a symptom? If the latter, what are the underlying influences? We investigated these questions with a series of tests that allowed for the generally very powerful effect of an establishment's workforce size.

One characteristic which appeared to have no influence upon the use of specialists at either board or establishment level was the production technology. This was categorized into the groups used by Daniel (1976) deriving from the work of Woodward (1965) and others. The differences to be found between the different technologies were insignificant when workforce size was allowed for. But a characteristic of the establishment that was very important was whether or not it was a part of a multi-plant firm. The probability of there being a director with industrial relations his sole responsibility was, for example, twice as great for establishments with 500 or more employees if they were part of multi-establishment firms than if they were single and independent. This is clearly illustrated by Table 3.2 with its industrial analysis. The industries at opposite extremes in their propensity to have industrial relations directors are food and clothing; they are also at opposite extremes in their propensity to have multi-plant firms.

A further analysis that we have conducted leaves no doubt that what is being detected here is the additional impact of enterprise size as opposed to establishment size. The results will be published elsewhere but an indication of them is given by the finding that, taking only

Management and Disputes Procedures

TABLE 3.1

ASPECTS OF MANAGEMENT BY ESTABLISHMENT SIZE

(Brackets indicate results based on cells with fewer than 20 cases in sample.)

	All Manu-factur-ing	Number of Full-Time Employees				
		50–99	100–199	200–499	500–999	1000+
Percent of Establishments:						
Specialist IR manager on site	46.2	21	40	78	92	95
Director responsible for IR	67.4	65	66	67	76	88
Director solely responsible for IR	29.8	19	27	39	52	69
IR function 'much more important'	35.8	24	32	53	57	55
Increased legislation seen as important	57.5	43	59	75	72	67
Single and independent establishment	27.7	34	33	18	12	5
Percentage of Subsidiaries:						
With IR function at higher level	70.6	57	80	73	81	86
'Complete' discretion in general IR	58.0	75	51	50	43	40
Percent of Specialist IR Managers 'Very Satisfied' that Management Generally:						
heeds IR procedures etc	58.7	(57)	62	60	58	52
seeks appropriate IR advice	65.5	(64)	72	64	63	60
passes on relevant information	56.9	(59)	66	54	52	46
IR Considerations Felt to Enter Centrally or Heavily in Decisions on:						
fixed capital investment	24.0	33	12	19	25	31
major method changes	39.9	39	35	43	46	59
redundancy	60.1	43	62	76	84	94
wages and conditions	61.0	43	63	79	85	96

TABLE 3.2

ASPECTS OF MANAGEMENT BY INDUSTRY

					Per cent of Establishments						
	All Manufac- turing	Food Drink Tobacco	Chemicals etc.	Metal Manufac- turing	Mechanical Engineering and Ships	Instrument and Electrical Engineering	Vehicles	Metal Goods N.E.S.	Textiles	Clothing Footwear etc.	Bricks, Timber, and Misc.	Paper Printing and Pub- lishing
Director with responsibility for IR	67.4	92	61	67	68	62	92	56	79	39	59	74
Director with sole responsibility for IR	29.8	71	39	28	27	41	55	27	14	10	16	22
Single, independent establishment	27.7	13	23	20	26	14	15	28	19	48	41	41
IR function has become 'much more important' in last 5 years	35.8	44	29	50	34	56	52	42	27	27	28	20
Increased legislation seen as prime cause of more important IR function	57.5	70	66	58	61	51	52	41	41	73	56	68

establishments with 500 or more employees, a director with industrial relations as his sole responsibility exists for 55 per cent of those in companies of fewer than 5,000 employees but for 81 per cent of those in companies of 5,000 employees or more. Large companies are more likely than small ones to have specialised industrial relations management.

Nor is it only at board level that company size affects the degree of management specialisation. The presence of a specialist director was closely correlated with there being a specialist respondent at establishment level. The latter were, for a given establishment size, more common in multi-plant firms than in independent establishments. Thus company size influences the degree of specialisation at establishment level.

There was much greater likelihood of foreign-owned firms having specialist directors and management than the British owned. A director with sole responsibilities in industrial relations was reported by 47 per cent of foreign-owned establishments but only 28 per cent of British, and the respondent was a specialist for 76 per cent of the former compared with only 43 per cent of the latter.

Less strong but still notable was the fact that, again allowing for size, establishments in membership of employers' associations were less likely to have either sort of specialist. Thirty-five per cent of non-members had directors with sole industrial relations responsibilities compared with 28 per cent of members; for specialist respondents the respective figures were 55 per cent and 44 per cent. It is a finding consistent with the Donovan assertion that membership of an employers' association might inhibit the development of a firm's industrial relations policy.

Perhaps most significant is the association between a firm's having a director with sole responsibility for industrial relations and its relying upon some sort of corporate arrangement (single-employer and multi-plant) for fixing manual workers' pay. Fifty per cent of establishments with corporate manual pay bargaining had specialist directors, compared with 32 per cent of those relying on establishment bargaining, 29 per cent relying on multi-employer agreements (including wages councils), and only 5 per cent of those with no pay bargaining at all. It was an association that applied irrespective of establishment size. It applied when corporate bargainers were compared with the others among multi-plant establishments, and also when they were compared with others among single-employer bargainers. Interestingly enough, there does not appear to be any association between corporate bargaining and a specialist industrial relations respondent.

What of the trade union side of the relationship? Could it be that management is obliged to develop specialised industrial relations roles in response to bargaining pressure? Discriminant analysis showed trade union density to be positively associated with specialist directors. There was also a clear tendency, irrespective of establishment size, for shop stewards to be more likely to hold regular steward meetings where there was a specialist director, and where we had a specialist respondent. Furthermore, a specialist director was also strongly associated with the existence of a full-time shop steward, although the association did not hold for a specialist respondent. But this does not tell us anything about the direction of causation; professional industrial relations management is at least as likely to encourage professional shop steward organisation as the other way round.

A clearer test of the hypothesis is given by strike experience, since management is unlikely to specialise in order to encourage strikes whereas a high strike incidence might encourage management specialisation. Considering separately five different size-bands of establishment, there was no evidence of any significant association between experience of a strike of a day or more and either a director with industrial relations among his responsibilities or a specialist respondent. There was a weak tendency in three size-bands for strike experience to be associated with a director with industrial relations as his sole reponsibility. There is thus no substantial support for the view that managerial specialisation is a response or, for that matter, a stimulant to an unusual level of strife in an establishment, just as these data would not support the view that managerial specialisation has any straightforward effect in creating peace.

In sum, a firm's decision to have specialist industrial relations management, while in broad terms a response to collective bargaining pressure, does not seem to be a simple reaction to an unusually difficult industrial problem. It arises from the overall size of the firm, from a certain preference for managerial division of labour which may be greater with overseas ownership, and above all from the decision to conduct bargaining within the company and at a level higher than the individual establishment.

Changes in the Degree of Specialisation

Some indication of the change that has occurred in the specialisation of industrial relations management can be gleaned from comparisons with previous surveys. Differences in definition and sampling technique, it should be stressed, make such comparisons extremely crude. The survey carried out in 1966 for the Donovan Commission found that 38 per cent of the manufacturing establishments it sampled had personnel officers with some responsibility for 'dealing with trade unions' (Government

Social Survey, 1968: 72—4). On a more restricted definition our broadly comparable 1978 figure is 46 per cent. Marsh's engineering survey of 1968/9 gives the proportion of establishments with personnel managers and also the proportion of these who negotiated with trade union officers (Marsh, 1971: 19). It implies that 55 per cent of establishments had such people; our sample of engineering establishments, including a much higher proportion of small plants and using a more restrictive definition, suggested a 1978 figure of 56 per cent. Finally, Parker's 1972 survey gives figures to suggest that 61 per cent of manufacturing establishments of over 250 employees had a separate personnel staff with industrial relations functions (Parker, 1974: A24). Our 1978 survey had a respondent whose specialisation was industrial relations in 85 per cent of establishments of comparable size. In short, making all due statistical allowances, it is highly likely that there has been a substantial increase in the degree of specialisation of industrial relations management at the workplace.

At the level of the board, definitions are more clear-cut. Marsh's engineering survey of 1968/9 had found that 41 per cent of companies had a director with personnel among his responsibilities; it was sole responsibility in 9 per cent (Marsh, 1971: 16). A British Institute of Management survey of the whole private sector carried out in 1971 found that 28 per cent of boards of directors have someone who had personnel matters among his responsibilities (BIM, 1972: 20). The 970 establishments in our 1978 survey came from 610 companies. Respondents from 74 per cent of these companies reported a director with some industrial relations responsibility; the proportion reporting it to be his sole responsibility was 42 per cent. The figures for engineering alone are likely to be slightly higher. Even allowing for the substantial differences in sampling methods, these data suggest that the 1970s have seen a very substantial increase in the responsibility taken for industrial relations by boards of directors.

Another way of enquiring into the question was to ask for the respondents' subjective impressions. We asked them whether they thought 'that the position of the industrial relations function here, in the last five years' had changed in importance. There is, perhaps, a natural tendency for an incumbent to consider his position to have grown in importance, but the unanimity of response was remarkable. Thirty-six per cent said that the industrial relations function had become 'much more important', 46 per cent that it had become 'more important', and only 17 per cent that it had 'stayed about the same'. An insignificant number said that it had 'become less important'.

Respondents from the larger establishments were much more likely to comment on the function's increased importance. As Table 3.1 shows, over half the establishments with workforces of 200 or more reported that the industrial relations function had become much more important. There was no strong association between this impression of recent change with multi-plant firms, with corporate bargaining, or with the presence of full-time shop stewards. Instead it was strongly associated with specialist industrial relations management at the workplace and on the board. There is thus confirmatory evidence of the rising status and numbers of specialist industrial relations management.

An initially paradoxical finding is that, for all size categories except workforces of 1,000 or more, there was a strong association between a 'much more important' industrial relations function and recent experience of a strike of a day or more. It thus appears that although, as the previous section noted, specialist industrial relations management was not particularly associated with strike-prone factories, it may be strike experience that stimulates an initial specialisation or that specialisation initially stimulates strikes.

Although, as Table 3.2 shows, the perception of a more important industrial relations function was reported particularly from the metals, engineering and food industries, it was generally widespread. We asked the four in five of respondents who reported it an open-ended question: 'Why do you think this is?'. The answers were interesting. About a quarter referred to management causes: 24 per cent to company policy of some sort and 4 per cent to the consequences of company growth. Somewhat fewer suggested that the explanation came from the union side: 13 per cent noted increased union power and demands, and 5 per cent reported that their domestic unions had arrived, been recognised, or grown during the previous five years. Another 12 per cent saw a national trend towards greater industrial democracy and participation as being important. But by far the largest proportion, 57 per cent, gave the cause as the increase in legislation.

In the eyes of our respondents, therefore, the most important cause of the rising importance of the industrial relations function in recent years has been the government's increased intervention. As the tables show, this was reported more from medium to larger size establishments and from the food and clothing industries. It was also more closely associated with respondents from single and independent, as opposed to multi-plant, establishments, from places which relied on industry-wide agreements for their manual pay rather than any other arrangement, from places which reported above average reliance upon full-time trade union officers, and which tended to have higher density of manual unionisation. There was no clear relationship with strike experience. It was associated with foreign-owned firms and establishments with specialist respondents. Perhaps most significant, increased legislation was the cause given by no less than 70 per cent of the respondents who said that the industrial relations function had become 'much more important' in the previous five years. It seems safe to conclude, therefore, that government intervention has had a profound effect in stimulating the increased specialisation of industrial relations management.

The Discretion Allowed to Subsidiaries

Almost three-quarters of manufacturing establishments of 50 or more employees are not single and independent, but are a part of a multi-plant enterprise. Table 3.1 shows that the larger an establishment is, the less likely it is to be single and independent; while a third of establishments with between 50 and 199 employees have this status, it applies to only one in twenty of those with a thousand or more employees. Put another way, it is not only the fact of its own size that makes for more complex industrial relations in a large establishment than a small one; it is also the fact that it is more likely to be a part of a larger enterprise.

There are profound implications for the conduct of collective bargaining in the extent to which the managements of subsidiary establishments are allowed discretion on industrial relations matters. This is particularly the case in Britain where reliance upon workplace bargaining is so great and the position of the shop steward is of such significance. There are no simple indicators that one can use for the degree of centralisation of decision-making in an organisation. Selecting only those establishments which were part of multi-plant firms but were not the British headquarters of the entire organisation, we asked first whether there was 'a specific personnel and industrial relations function at some higher level in the group or organisation'. Our second approach was to ask the respondents' impressions of the amount of discretion that management at their establishment had over settling matters concerned with a range of industrial relations issues.

For 71 per cent of the subsidiaries there was a specialist personnel and industrial relations function at some higher level. As Table 3.1 shows, this was less common for establishments with fewer than 100 employees. It was more common with foreign than British-owned subsidiaries. But the strongest correlate was that of the bargaining arrangements used. Where manual pay was primarily fixed at establishment level, 67 per cent of respondents reported a specialist function higher than their workplace. For multi-employer arrangements the figure was 72 per cent and for an absence of any bargaining it was 66 per cent. But where there was corporate bargaining over manual pay (defined, it will be recalled, as an arrangement with a single firm covering more than one but not necessarily all establishments), there were specialist functions at a higher level for 87 per cent of establishments.

Presumably reflecting the association of higher level specialist functions with corporate arrangements, there was a tendency for the reported reliance upon full-time trade union officers to be greater where there was a higher level specialist. Where there was no higher specialist, the proportion of respondents saying that the role of the full-time officer was 'not very' or 'not at all' important was 51 per cent; where the higher level specialist was present the proportion was 42 per cent. A rise in the locus of management decision-making above the workplace appears to be linked with a similar move on the union side.

The issues chosen for an investigation of the subsidiary managements' impression of their discretion covered both individual and collective matters: training policy, manual workers' pay, junior management pay, redundancies, dismissals, and 'industrial relations matters generally'. Respondents were asked how much discretion they felt that management at their establishment had over settling matters concerned with these issues: 'complete or almost complete freedom', 'considerable discretion within broadly defined rules or advice', 'limited discretion within fairly detailed rules', or 'virtually no freedom'. The first part of Table 3.3 gives the breakdown of all responses across these categories of discretion for each issue.

It is clear that the degree of discretion varies substantially according to the issue. Dismissals are left almost entirely to the local management. Training policy (which includes apprenticeships) and general industrial relations matters (which presumably cover day-to-day consultation and conflict management) tend to receive more guidance from above. There is substantially less likelihood that redundancy matters will be left to the discretion of the local management: for a substantial proportion there is no discretion at all. Least latitude of all is on matters of pay. If anything, junior management pay is even more tightly controlled than manual pay although there is surprisingly little difference between the two. Perhaps most significant is the wide variation in control over pay allowed to different subsidiaries.

For an explanation of the variation between establishments it is natural to turn first to their firms' choice of bargaining arrangements. The second half of Table 3.3 analyses the responses, giving for each cell the proportion reporting 'complete or almost complete freedom'. It comes as little surprise that it is establishments where manual pay is

TABLE 3.3

THE DEGREE OF DISCRETION IN SUBSIDIARY PLANTS

issues	degree of discretion – % giving each response				principal arrangement for manual wage fixing – % saying 'complete or almost complete freedom'			
	complete or almost complete	considerable discretion within broadly defined rules or advice	limited discretion within fairly detailed rules	virtually no freedom	multi-employer agreement	corporate agreement	establishment agreement	no bargaining
training policy	60	32	5	2	65	34	61	84
manual workers' pay	33	34	19	14	32	19	34	51
junior management pay	33	29	20	16	36	20	31	45
redundancies	40	28	16	9	40	22	46	30
dismissals	74	17	7	1	74	63	74	85
industrial relations matters generally	58	32	8	–	71	29	51	91

determined by corporate agreements that have least discretion on all issues. And, while it may be a little odd that the freedom of control claimed for manual pay under corporate agreements is not even lower, it is remarkable that the degree of external control over training, redundancies and general industrial relations is also very high. Corporate bargaining on manual pay, we may conclude, tends to be associated with centralisation over a much wider range of issues than pay.

It is interesting to note how little difference there is in the profile of discretion between subsidiaries covered by multi-employer industry agreements and those relying primarily on establishment bargaining. Only on general industrial relations matters do they differ substantially, with the establishment bargainers receiving more guidance from above. That multi-employer agreements should appear to have so small an effect upon a manager's sense of discretion on both pay and non-pay matters is confirmation of their predominant weakness. Where there is no bargaining at all the subsidiary management reports more discretion on all issues but redundancies; one might surmise that a total absence of union resistance permits a more centralised company manpower policy.

Bargaining structure is clearly a powerful determinant of local managerial discretion. All the generalisations distinguishing the corporate bargainers from the rest were sustained when tests were carried out to allow for the effects of establishment size. But there are additional characteristics which appear to be associated with perceived discretion. One is size itself. The larger a subsidiary is, the less discretion it is felt to have and, although the effect is weak on pay and redundancy matters (and non-existent on dismissal), it is stronger on training and general industrial relations matters (illustrated in Table 3.1). Large subsidiaries appear to be more likely than small ones to have training and industrial relations guidance from on high.

Managerial specialisation outside the establishment is associated with a substantial reduction in local discretion on all issues but dismissal. Allowing for size effects, the presence of a director responsible for industrial relations, and of an industrial relations function higher in the firm (and the two are closely related) appear to reduce local discretion. And, since they are also associated with a specialist respondent at the establishment itself, there is the nice paradox that the presence of a senior industrial relations specialist within the establishment tends to be associated with a low level of establishment discretion. The local man, it seems, acts more as a commissar for company policy than as a decision-maker in his own right. Local discretion is consistently less in foreign than in British-owned establishments. Allowing for plant size there is little systematic difference between industries, or between different production technologies.

If we turn to the indicators of trade union organisation, the picture is revealing, if rather faint. There is no simple relationship with density of unionisation. The presence of a full-time shop steward tended to be associated with substantially less local discretion, particularly in the larger plants and, less clearly, the association with regular shop steward meetings was the same. Still allowing for size effects, the experience of a strike of a day or more tended to be associated with less local management discretion (on all matters other than redundancy) than where such a strike had not occurred.

Drawing conclusions from these relationships is far from easy. The measure of discretion is subjective and a manager who is under trade union pressure is more likely to be aware of the limits to his discretion than one who is not. Certainly it appears to be the case that managers feel themselves to have less discretion in subsidiaries with active and strike-prone workforces than in those where the workforce is more docile. There may be no evidence here for the view that a strong workforce tends to squeeze flexibility out of its local management. But, equally, it would be rash to adopt with any confidence the opposite view that a company's response to workplace bargaining is to lift managerial discretion out of workplace reach.

What changes in discretion have been taking place? We asked our respondents in subsidiaries whether, during the previous five years, they had felt that the amount of discretion allowed to management at their establishment by the wider organisation had increased, stayed the same, or decreased. This was asked with respect to first, pay and, second, other terms and conditions of employment. It should be added that these five years had witnessed the reintroduction of at times strict incomes policy.

Most notable about the responses was their diversity. An increase in discretion over pay was reported by 22 per cent of subsidiaries: a decrease by 21 per cent. For discretion over matters of terms and conditions an increase was reported by 25 per cent and a decrease by 14 per cent. There are no very clear patterns. Establishments reporting that the importance of their industrial relations function has increased in recent years divide fairly evenly between those reporting increasing and those reporting decreasing discretion. Corporate bargaining tends to be linked to a decrease in discretion as does recent strike experience. The overall impression is of neither universal nor uniform organisational change: increased specialisation does not necessarily imply increased centralisation.

Industrial Relations Managers' Satisfaction with Management

The fact that a management has devoted more specialised resources to industrial relations matters does not necessarily mean that it makes use of them. At those establishments where the respondent was a personnel or industrial relations specialist we asked how satisfied he was with three aspects of his relationship with local management. First, whether they generally took heed of industrial relations policies, procedures and agreements. Second, whether they sought appropriate advice from him or his department on industrial relations matters. Third, whether they generally passed on relevant information to him and his department about events at the establishment. The responses were categorised as 'very', 'fairly', 'not very' and 'not at all' satisfied.

The majority of respondents reported themselves to be very satisfied in all three respects. Two-thirds (65 per cent) were very satisfied that management generally sought appropriate advice on industrial relations matters and 59 per cent and 57 per cent respectively were equally happy with the extent to which heed was taken of industrial relations policies and relevant information was passed on. The great bulk of the remaining responses were in the 'fairly satisfied' category with a few 'not at all' responses only on the question of the passing on of information.

This satisfaction tended, however, to diminish with increasing establishment size. As Table 3.1 shows, this size effect is particularly marked in the case of the relevant information being passed on; less than half the industrial relations managers with workforces of 1,000 or more were very satisfied in this respect and 10 per cent were 'not very' or 'not at all satisfied'.

There are so many other characteristics of an establishment's industrial relations that also vary systematically with its workforce size that it is difficult, without much larger samples, to distinguish the one most closely related to this effect. Allowing for size there were significant signs that satisfaction with the rest of management in all three respects was less where there had been experience of strikes of a day or more than where there had not. More unevenly, regular steward meetings were associated with reduced satisfaction, and full-time stewards specifically with less satisfaction with relevant information being passed on. As was the case with the question of managerial discretion, this subjective indicator should be interpreted with caution. The greater bargaining pressure an industrial relations manager is under, the greater are likely to be his demands upon his fellow managers. If, as appears, he is less satisfied with the quality of the information he gets in a factory with a full-time shop steward, a large part of the explanation is likely to come from the fact that the existence of a full-time steward improves intelligence on the trade union side.

The existence of higher level specialist support appeared to influence the manager's satisfaction only with respect to receiving relevant information from other managers. Both an industrial relations director and a specialist at a higher level outside the establishment appeared, with size allowed for, to help the local manager in this respect. There were no important differences when industry and production technology were examined.

As before, however, a company's bargaining arrangements seemed to have a substantial effect. Sample sizes were too small to consider places where there was no bargaining, but of the other arrangements, satisfaction was markedly less where there was corporate bargaining. On the question of management heeding industrial relations policies, 68 per cent declared themselves very satisfied from plants covered by multi-employer agreements, 61 per cent with establishment bargaining, but only 45 per cent where the agreement was corporate. There was less difference on the matter of seeking appropriate advice: the figures were respectively 65 per cent, 67 per cent, and 62 per cent. On the passing on of relevant information they were respectively 62 per cent, 57 per cent, and 45 per cent. If, as suggested earlier, the industrial relations manager of a plant covered by a corporate agreement acts more as a commissar for externally determined policies than as a local negotiator, there are likely to be many more causes of friction between him and his local management.

The Centrality of Industrial Relations Considerations

What influences the priority that industrial relations considerations are given in the total process of management? So far this chapter has focused on industrial relations management, its degree of specialisation, the discretion allowed to it, and the extent to which it feels well used by other management functions. To place the discussion in a broader perspective we now consider where industrial relations factors stand in relation to other elements influencing managerial decisions. Recent research into organisational behaviour has suggested that, looking through the eyes of the key decision-makers, industrial relations factors stand rather far down the list (Hickson and Mallory, 1980). Certainly the discussion in Chapter 2 detected no straight-forward industrial relations rationale for the type of internal bargaining structure that a multi-plant company adopts. But here we are concerned with how priorities look through the eyes of the manager at establishment level responsible for industrial relations, and with how these subjective impressions vary with different circumstances.

We asked respondents how influential they thought personnel and industrial relations *considerations* were in formulating policy and making decisions in their organisation on four different issues. The issues were: fixed capital investment decisions, major changes in production methods, wages and conditions of employment, and decisions to make employees redundant. They were asked to say whether these considerations played the central role, were heavily involved, were subjects of consultation, or were not involved at all. In the following discussion we consider the percentage of responses which said that the considerations were 'central', or 'heavily involved' (abbreviated to 'important').

Personnel and industrial relations considerations were held to be important to decisions on fixed capital investment by only 24 per cent of respondents, but they were thought important to major changes in production methods by 40 per cent. The figures for terms and conditions of employment and redundancy were much higher at, respectively, 61 per cent and 60 per cent. As is evident from Table 3.1, there is a general tendency for the perceived importance of industrial relations considerations to increase with establishment size; it is particularly clear-cut for wages and conditions. The bigger the workplace, it appears, the greater the priority that those responsible for industrial relations feel that management gives to their subject. Added to this, the size of the company as a whole appears to be important. The effect is stronger in multi-plant than in single establishments.

Is the weight given to industrial relations considerations a reflection of the specialism of management or of the magnitude of the problems presented by the workforce? There is certainly strong evidence that specialist industrial relations management is associated with high priority being given to the subject. Compared with those establishments where the roles do not exist, industrial relations considerations were ascribed much greater importance on each issue (except that of changes in production methods) where there was a specialist respondent and specialist director. There was no clear connection with the presence of a specialist function higher than the establishment. All these tests were carried out allowing for workforce size effects. Breakdowns by technology and industry showed no clear associations.

Bargaining arrangements once again appeared to be influential. Although the results defy simple summary, the outstanding one, allowing for establishment size, was that much higher priority was thought to be given to industrial relations matters where there was corporate bargaining than where there was not. Using our indicator for importance this does not show up clearly for capital investment decisions, but it does for the other three issues. Overall, the average proportion ascribing importance on method changes was 40 per cent; for those with a corporate arrange-

ment it was 59 per cent. For the whole sample on wages and conditions
it was 61 per cent, but 72 per cent for those with corporate arrangements.
On redundancy the figures were 60 per cent and 85 per cent respectively.
There seems little doubt that industrial relations considerations are felt
to weigh heavier with management where there is a corporate agreement
than where there is not.

Shop steward organisation also carried some explanatory weight. There
was substantially more consideration ascribed to industrial relations
matters on all four issues (workforce size allowed for) where there was
a full-time shop steward than where there was not. The holding of regular
steward meetings appeared to hold an association for all but redundancy
questions. Perhaps most interesting was the link with strike experience.
Strikes of a day or more were strongly associated with above average
emphasis on industrial relations considerations on investment decisions
and on changes in production methods, but not at all with the other two
issues.

Some disentangling of these findings comes if we consider the relative
strength of the effects. On questions of capital investment and production
method changes it is the indicators of trade union organisation and
strength that appear to have a stronger effect than those of management
specialisation. On the more normal industrial relations areas of wages and
conditions and redundancy it is the other way round. On all four areas
corporate bargaining appears to be important. We might conclude tenta-
tively, first, that management gives higher priority to industrial relations
considerations on orthodox industrial relations questions if there is
specialist management. Second, that industrial relations considerations
enter into decisions of wider management significance if the workforce is
powerful enough to impose its views. Third, that management pays heed
to industrial relations considerations across the range of issues if, via a
corporate bargaining arrangement, the wider organisation obliges it to do
so.

Disputes Procedures

Disputes procedures provide a framework within which workplace
industrial relations are conducted. By specifying the individuals or committees to be involved in dispute resolution, and the sequence in which
they are to be involved, a procedure defines a pattern of authority for
both management and employees. It was a central assertion of the
Donovan Commission that a major cause of industrial strife in Britain was
procedural disarray. Because managements were reluctant to acknowledge
the *de facto* pattern of bargaining and, in particular, the key role of shop

stewards, the *de jure* procedures for dispute resolution failed to involve the right people. Confusion and disagreement resulted which, the Commission urged, could only be resolved by the agreement of company and factory disputes procedures that brought a better match between power and authority (Royal Commission, 1968: 45).

During the subsequent decade substantial government pressures were directed to this end. Starting with *In Place of Strife* (1969) and then the *Industrial Relations Code of Practice* (1971) employers were urged to formalise procedures for negotiating arrangements as well as for collective disputes, individual grievances and disciplinary mtters. The Commission on Industrial Relations was established in large part to facilitate the process. Legislation has also encouraged the development of certain procedures. Employees are now entitled to be told, within 13 weeks of appointment, how they can seek redress of any individual grievance and disciplinary decision relating to their employment. The introduction of statutory protection against unfair dismissal in 1971 (subsequently amended), which involves consideration of the *manner* of dismissal as well as the reason has given a particular stimulus to the introduction of discipline and dismissal procedures. The Advisory, Conciliation and Arbitration Service has produced a more detailed code of practice.

We wanted to find out the extent of disputes procedures and how far they involved the use of third party intervention. Our questions distinguished three types of procedure — for handling disputes about individual grievances, about discipline or dismissal, and about pay and conditions — although in practice these tend to be closely inter-related, with individual grievances sometimes developing into collective disputes. In 70 per cent of cases the procedure for handling disputes about discipline or dismissal was the same as the individual grievance procedure. We asked whether procedures were written down or based upon oral understandings. We also sought to ascertain how far they were the result of negotiations with trade unions and how far management had introduced them unilaterally.

A survey of this sort is a weak instrument with which to explore these questions. The existence of a written procedure in an establishment is far from being a guarantee that disputes are actually processed in the prescribed way. In some establishments there will be a network of informal paths around the formal one and the choice between them will depend upon, among other things, the strength of the workers' organisation, the nature of the bargaining relationships and the issue at stake. To ascertain how procedures really work it is necessary to carry out detailed case studies (Thomson and Murray, 1976). But, although our questions tell us far from the whole story, they do provide a systematic starting point.

A very high proportion of establishments reported that they had procedures. Pay and conditions procedures were reported for 87 per cent of establishments, procedures for disputes about discipline or dismissal (other than redundancy) were reported for 89 per cent, and procedures to deal with individual grievances for 92 per cent. Because the introduction of a procedure is rarely a once-and-for-all-time event it was impractical to ask their age. Instead some rough indication of the changing pattern of procedures can be gained by a comparison with the Government Social Survey study of 1966 (1968: 82). Works managers in establishments of at least 150 employees had been asked about formal procedures for dealing with 'claims and grievances' within the establishment. Of those not members of an employers' association, 76 per cent had such a procedure and, of those who were members, 59 per cent said that 'in addition to national procedure, they had their own formal plant procedure' (65 per cent in metal handling trades and 62 per cent in other manufacturing). A survey in 1972 suggested a figure closer to 50 per cent for written workplace procedures (Parker, 1974: 32). There are several definitional and sampling problems that prevent a precise comparison, but in broad terms our own survey suggests that by 1978 there were workplace procedures in 95 per cent, and written workplace procedures in 80 per cent, of similarly sized establishments. While hesitating to place a magnitude on it, we can say with confidence that the 1970s saw a very substantial increase in all forms of disputes procedures.

The uniformly high incidence of the different sorts of procedure across different industries is shown in Table 4.4. The chemicals industry is notable for its lower proportion of pay and conditions procedures and textiles for the greater scarcity of the other two types. But it is workforce size rather than the specific attributes of industries that probably provides a more useful association between an establishment and the existence of a procedure. Table 3.5 shows that, particularly when the workforce size is below 100, there is markedly less likelihood of each of the three types of procedure being present.

There is, however, a stronger relationship underlying this association of workforce size with the presence of procedures. Both are associated with the density of unionisation, and discriminant analysis showed the relationship of procedures with union density to be stronger than their relationship with workforce size. Pay and conditions procedures were present in 74 per cent of establishments where less than 60 per cent of the manual workforce was unionised, but in 92 per cent where 60 per cent or more was unionised. Procedures were almost universal where there was a full-time shop steward. They were also more likely to be found in establishments which had past experience of strike action than in those which had not.

TABLE 3.4

PROCEDURES AND THIRD PARTY INTERVENTION BY INDUSTRY

	Percentage of Establishments											
	All Manufacturing	Food Drink Tobacco	Chemicals etc.	Metal Manufacturing	Mechanical Engineering and Ships	Instrument and Electrical Engineering	Vehicles	Metal Goods N.E.S.	Textiles	Clothing Footwear etc.	Bricks, Timber, and Misc.	Paper Printing and Publishing
Existence of pay and conditions procedure	87.1	98	76	99	80	97	99	92	90	91	73	80
Existence of discipline or dismissal disputes procedure	88.6	99	95	90	89	93	91	96	64	81	87	94
Existence of individual grievance procedure	91.7	99	100	95	89	99	90	82	64	99	88	84
Percent of pay and conditions procedures with outside intervention	37.1	58	71	43	32	32	40	36	36	20	33	27
Percent of discipline or dismissal disputes procedures with outside intervention	21.0	41	32	20	22	21	15	16	19	17	20	7
Percent of individual grievance procedure with outside intervention	20.8	41	29	15	21	20	25	13	21	13	20	10

TABLE 3.5

CHARACTERISTICS OF PROCEDURES BY WORKFORCE SIZE

	Percentage of Establishments by Number of Full-Time Employees				
	50–99	100–199	200–499	500–999	1000+
Existence of procedure:					
Pay and conditions	81	88	92	96	99
Discipline or dismissal disputes	77	96	96	97	97
Individual grievance	80	98	97	98	99
Per cent with outside intervention:					
Pay and conditions	23	42	47	53	50
Discipline or dismissal disputes	12	21	31	31	26
Individual grievance	11	21	31	30	29
Per cent written:					
Pay and conditions*	76	71	85	88	88
Discipline or dismissal disputes	75	72	81	86	83
Individual grievance	86	69	76	84	87
Per cent negotiated:					
Pay and conditions*	78	63	79	81	85
Discipline or dismissal disputes	75	72	81	86	83
Individual grievance	29	59	73	67	75

* The slight difference in coverage of this question is described in the text.

Several management characteristics are also associated with procedures. Foreign owned establishments were almost without exception in having all three forms of procedure in contrast to their British owned counterparts. Multi-plant establishments were more likely to have procedures than those that were independent. Membership of an employers' association and the type of pay bargaining structure, on the other hand, did not appear to have any substantial effect. In the previous chapter it was noted that two-thirds of establishments that were members of employers' associations were aware of their association having an external disputes procedure; its presence does not appear to affect the likelihood of their having an internal procedure.

About three-quarters of procedures were reported to be written down, although with what degree of precision we are unable to say. For discipline and dismissals the figure was 77 per cent, for individual grievances it was 74 per cent, and for pay and conditions it was 79 per cent (although this last figure relates only to procedures with third party intervention). As can be seen from Table 3.5, the larger the size of the workforce the more likely are procedures to be written. The same size relationship (probably reflecting aspects of union organisation) can be seen to apply to whether a procedure was said to have been negotiated as opposed to unilaterally introduced by management. Sixty-four per cent of discipline and dismissal procedures were reported to have been negotiated, 57 per cent of individual grievance procedures, and, again, relating only to those with third party intervention, 75 per cent of pay and conditions procedures.

Third Party Intervention

When the provisions of an internal procedure fail to resolve a matter it may be placed in an external procedure, most commonly operated by an employers' association and trade unions. It was reported in the previous chapter that almost half of the establishments which said that their association offered such a procedure had made use of it during the preceding two years. Whether or not such a procedure is used, a third party may be called in. He may conciliate by assisting the parties to reach their own settlement. He may mediate by making proposals for the employer and union protagonists to accept or reject. Or he may arbitrate by making a decision to which the parties have agreed to be bound. In practice the parties may wish to use more than one of these functions. There has been a marked increase in interest in the use of third party intervention in Britain during the last decade with the creation of the Advisory, Conciliation and Arbitration Service.

A minority of procedures provide for outside intervention. Asked whether their procedures had provision for intervention by ACAS or by some body other than an employers' association or trade union, 37 per cent of establishments said that they had for pay and conditions, 21 per cent for discipline or dismissal, and 21 per cent also for individual grievances. As Table 3.4 shows, there are differences between industries. The food, drink and tobacco and the chemicals industries appear to have well above average provision for third party intervention while in the paper and printing industry this is notable for its comparative rarity.

Larger establishments are, as Table 3.5 shows, more likely to have third party intervention provisions. As with the existence of procedures, this association appears to spring in large part from a stronger underlying association with density of trade union membership. Where less than 60 per cent of the manual workforce was unionised there were provisions for intervention in only 27 per cent of pay and conditions procedures compared with such provision in 43 per cent of procedures where 60 per cent or more was unionised. Third party provisions were less common where there had been no recent experience of strikes.

There were some specific management characteristics associated with the provision of third party intervention. Foreign-owned firms showed a marked preference for it by comparison with the British-owned. It was common where there was single employer as opposed to multi-employer wage bargaining, and particularly where there was corporate bargaining. Its provision appeared to be inhibited slightly by membership of an employers' association. Possibly the external procedure provided by most employers' associations provides a satisfactory substitute for non-partisan intervention.

There is, of course, no certainty that a provision for third party intervention will be used. We asked the minority of establishments with such a provision whether it had been used during the previous two years. Twenty-one per cent said it had been for pay and conditions disputes, 8 per cent for discipline or dismissal disputes, and 5 per cent for individual grievances. The food and clothing industries were outstanding for their high use of intervention in pay and conditions disputes. Discriminant analysis revealed use of intervention to be more common where there were larger workforces (presumably because it affects the number of disputes) and higher density of unionisation.

The absence of provisions for intervention in a procedure does not exclude the possibility of its use. Establishments with no provision were asked whether they had in fact used intervention from outside the industry during the previous two years: 4 per cent said they had for pay and conditions matters, 7 per cent for discipline or dismissal and 1 per cent for individual grievance. Thus it is very unusual for an establishment without provision for intervention to make use of it.

In practice the different forms of third party intervention are often used in conjunction with each other. Respondents with provision for intervention in their pay and conditions procedures were asked about its form. Eighty-five per cent said that it was for conciliation and/or mediation and 56 per cent said that it was for arbitration, figures implying that for almost a third the intervention could take either form. Of those who specified arbitration, 68 per cent said that it could not be arranged without agreement by both sides and only 19 per cent said that it could be initiated by one party alone.

What degree of success can be attributed to such intervention? In the case of pay and conditions procedures with third party provision, if intervention had been called upon, we asked whether the last case had been resolved. It had been for 64 per cent of cases. We could discern no factors which correlated with whether or not an establishment's last case of intervention had brought resolution of the dispute. When asked about their satisfaction with the experience respondents were generally positive. Thirty-eight per cent of them said that they were 'very' satisfied with the outcome, 37 per cent were 'fairly' satisfied, and only 18 per cent 'not very' and 2 per cent 'not at all' satisfied. Once again there were no clear correlates with the respondent's satisfaction, but, in so far as the types of intervention can be separated, it was conciliation rather than arbitration that was associated with the more satisfying outcome for management, a finding that is hardly surprising.

Overwhelmingly the most important provider of third party intervention, whether named in procedure or called upon in an *ad hoc* way, was ACAS. The Service was named in 85 per cent of pay and conditions procedures which had third party provision, 78 per cent of discipline and dismissal procedures, and 79 per cent of individual grievance procedures. It was called upon in 86 per cent of the relatively few *ad hoc* occasions. Overall, its intervention had led to the resolution of the dispute in 75 per cent of cases, and almost 75 per cent of respondents were either 'very', or 'fairly' satisfied with the outcome.

When asked whether they thought there was, in general terms, a need for some sort of independent conciliation and arbitration service in Britain, 81 per cent of respondents said that there was. When asked whether they regarded ACAS as independent, 56 per cent of all respondents considered it to be so. Of the 26 per cent who felt that it was not independent, the majority felt it to be biased towards trade unions (or employees); most of the remainder considered it to be an agency of government. The survey came at a time when the Grunwick troubles had brought ACAS under considerable public attack. The allegations of bias came particularly from respondents in the smaller establishments.

It is clear, in conclusion, that disputes procedures have spread rapidly during the 1970s to become part of the normal fabric of workplace industrial relations in manufacturing industry. Wherever there is a high level of unionisation there is likely to be a set of procedures, mostly written and arrived at through negotiation. On pay and conditions matters, about a third of these procedures have provision for third party intervention. These provisions had been used by a fifth of the establishments that had them during the two years before the survey. For two-thirds of cases the intervention had led to the resolution of the dispute, and for three-quarters management was satisfied with the outcome.

Is third party intervention becoming more popular in Britain? Goodman and Krislov (1974: 334) noted a 'gradual upward trend' in the number of conciliation cases dealt with by officers of the Department of Employment (and its predecessors) during the 1960s and they showed how it 'accelerated markedly in the early 1970s': the number of cases frose from an annual average of 439 for the years 1965—69 to 866 for 1973. Under the mantle of ACAS, the number of collective conciliation cases has remained fairly steady at a much higher level: 2284 cases in 1979 (ACAS, 1980). We have noted from our survey that very few uses of third party intervention in manufacturing occur outside procedural provisions and that the great majority of them call on ACAS as opposed to other agencies. We conclude that, after a possible surge when ACAS was created, there are no signs of a major swing to third party intervention on collective matters, despite the likelihood that procedural provision for it has been increasing.

Conclusion

This chapter has demonstrated that, during the past decade, manufacturing industry has carried out extensive procedural reform and has substantially raised the emphasis given to industrial relations management. These developments have been fully in line with the prescriptions of the Donovan Commission. How far the procedural innovations have been paper reforms is best assessed in the light of the next chapter's discussion of shop steward organisation. For the moment it is worth noting that one potential area of development in British collective bargaining, that of third party intervention in collective disputes, has not undergone any sustained expansion.

Two distinct developments appear to have encouraged the growing professionalism of industrial relations management. One has been the increase in government intervention in industrial relations, both legislative and otherwise, in recent years. This has demanded a level of expertise previously unknown in industrial relations management. The second has been the change in bargaining arrangements. Single-employer bargaining of itself has not had a particularly distinctive impact on the specialisation of industrial relations management; multi-employer agreements are generally fairly loose and require much the same sort of specialisation and discretion at the workplace as where the main level of bargaining is the establishment. But where it has been decided to carry out single-employer bargaining at a higher level than the individual establishment, the impact upon management is more distinct. In these circumstances of corporate bargaining a higher priority has been accorded to industrial relations at board level. The inevitable strains that come from binding diverse workplaces to the constraints of a multi-plant agreement are reflected in the lower discretion allowed to the local industrial relations manager and in his relatively poor relations with other management at the site.

4

Trade Union Organisation at the Workplace

An outstanding feature of post-war industrial relations in Britain has been the steady growth in the stature and extent of shop steward organisations. This growth has been strongly influenced by the developments outlined in the previous chapters: the spread of single-employer bargaining, the increased professionalism of industrial relations management and the reform of disputes procedures. A central concern of the study was where these had left the state of shop steward organisations in 1978. The fact that the present survey was directed at management obliged us to leave untouched the finer and less formal points of shop steward activities and to concentrate on the broad framework of workplace union organisation with which managers would be familiar.

In what follows we describe the extent of trade union membership and recognition, the closed shop, and multi-unionism. We then go on to the nature of shop steward organisations and their relationship with management and full-time union officials. Finally consideration is given to the forms of employee representation and consultation that occur outside normal trade union channels. The manual and non-manual parts of the workforce are discussed separately.

The Extent of Trade Union Membership

On the basis of managers' estimates for their own workplaces we calculate that 74 per cent of the full-time workforce in manufacturing establishments of at least 50 employees are members of trade unions. The densities of unionisation of the manual and non-manual parts of the workforce are, respectively, 82 per cent and 48 per cent. The previous most authoritative estimate of unionisation in manufacturing, by Price and Bain (1976), worked from aggregate union membership data for 1974; it provided an overall figure for that year of 62 per cent. When allowance is made for

TABLE 4.1

TRADE UNION PRESENCE IN THE ESTABLISHMENT BY INDUSTRY

(Percentages)

	All Manufacturing	Food, Drink, Tobacco	Chemicals etc.	Metal Manufacturing	Mechanical Engineering and Ships	Instrument, and Electrical Engineering	Vehicles	Metal Goods N.E.S.	Textiles	Clothing Leather, Footwear	Bricks, Timber and Misc.	Paper, Printing and Publishing
Manual												
Union recognised	75.7	91	69	95	67	64	87	76	57	77	77	87
Shop steward present	73.1	80	69	90	67	63	87	75	49	76	77	86
Percentage unionisation of industry workforce	82.3	88	83	94	82	74	94	78	62	70	80	94
Non-Manual												
Union recognised	36.3	38	30	48	47	49	46	34	19	21	35	34
Shop steward present	34.5	33	30	48	47	48	46	32	16	19	33	30
Percentage unionisation of industry workforce	47.6	45	41	62	49	41	69	42	29	27	39	47

their inclusion of managers, and of establishments of fewer than 50 employees, and also for the overall growth in union membership between the two estimates, our figure and theirs are in close accord.

TABLE 4.2

TRADE UNION PRESENCE IN THE ESTABLISHMENT BY WORKFORCE SIZE

(Percentages)

	Total	Number of full-time employees				
		50–99	100–199	200–499	500–999	1000+
Manual						
Union recognised	75.7	59	83	89	92	97
Shop stewards present	73.1	56	80	87	92	97
Average unionisation within establishments where unions are present	73.1	65	76	75	84	90
At least partial closed shop	29.5	16	29	41	49	70
More than one recognised union present	36.3	18	32	55	73	90
Non-Manual						
Union recognised	36.3	20	26	58	77	89
Shop stewards present	34.5	20	21	56	77	88
Average unionisation within establishments where unions are present	41.4	39	30	46	49	62
At least partial closed shop	6.1	4	2	7	14	28
More than one recognised union present	13.1	2	7	21	40	67

Trade union density by industry is given in Table 4.1. It also shows where one or more unions 'are recognised by management for negotiating pay and conditions'. The largest single factor contributing to variations in these indicators between industries is establishment size. Using these data, Bain and Elsheikh (1980) have accounted for 30 per cent of the variance in union density in terms of the reciprocal of establishment size; a measure indicating that the sensitivity of unionisation to size diminishes the larger the establishment. Table 4.2 shows how union recognition and the average density of unionisation increase with establishment size. The weaker response of the non-manual workforce than of the manual to increasing establishment size is in large part explained by the fact that, in the average manufacturing establishment, there are only a third as many non-manual as manual employees. They almost invariably negotiate and organise quite separately from each other and are thus likely to exhibit a different relationship with total establishment size.

The Closed Shop

One marked difference between manual and non-manual unionisation lies in the much greater dispersion of densities to be found among non-manual workforces. More than half (53 per cent) of establishments with manual unions present have over 90 per cent of their manual workforce in unions; by contrast, only 17 per cent of those with non-manual unions have over 90 per cent of their non-manual workforce unionised. Part of the explanation of this lies in the different incidence of the closed shop.

The closed shop is a complex phenomenon traditionally relying largely upon informal social pressures for its existence. It is, consequently, a difficult matter to explore through a survey and we used a question based upon McCarthy's definition (McCarthy, 1964) to establish its extent. Managers were asked: 'In practice do any manual (non-manual) workers here have to be union members in order to keep their jobs?' and, if so, what proportion of jobs fell into this category.

The replies permit us to calculate that 37 per cent of the total full-time, non-managerial workforce in manufacturing establishments of at least 50 employees are actually members of a closed shop. This breaks down into 46 per cent of manual and 10 per cent of non-manual employees. It implies that 50 per cent of trade unionists in manufacturing establishments of at least 50 employees are members of a closed shop: 55 per cent of manuals and 20 per cent of non-manuals.

It should be stressed that this estimate is derived from employers alone and that, especially where the closed shop arrangements are informal, it will tend to understate the extent of the practice. This certainly seems to be the case when our estimates are compared with those of Gennard, Dunn and Wright (1980), also for 1978. Using both management and union sources they produce a higher overall figure, although their profile of variations in the closed shop across industries is remarkably close to ours.

The only previous estimate of the extent of the closed shop is McCarthy's for 1962 (McCarthy, 1964). His figures suggest that the proportion of the total manufacturing workforce at that time included in closed shops was 25 per cent. If we make the assumption that the closed shop is all but insignificant in establishments employing fewer than 50 workers, our data suggest a comparable figure for 1978 of 31 per cent. The figures of Gennard, Dunn and Wright for 1978 suggest a minimum coverage of the closed shop in manufacturing of 39 per cent.

Over the sixteen years since McCarthy's survey the workforce in manufacturing industry has declined by 18 per cent, and some of the sharpest contraction has been in industries such as shipbuilding, steel, and heavy engineering, which were traditional strongholds of the closed shop. Probably because we only used management sources, our figures for the coverage of the closed shop in its traditional areas of metal working and printing (shown in Table 4.3) are lower than McCarthy's. What is noteworthy is the very substantial increase in the closed shop is apparent, irrespective of reporting bias, in industries where it was unusual in 1962. Comparing McCarthy's data with our own (and giving Gennard *et al.*'s figures for minimum coverage in brackets) the change between 1962 and 1978 is as follows: in textiles from 14 per cent to 18 per cent (21 per cent); in clothing and footwear from 6 per cent to 19 per cent (23 per cent); in chemicals and allied industries from 7 per cent to 32 per cent (32 per cent); in food, drink, and tobacco from 4 per cent to 39 per cent (38 per cent). The spread of the closed shop to new areas has more than compensated for the contraction of its traditional habitat.

The overall picture of the extent of the closed shop by industry is given in Table 4.3, where manual and non-manual employees are dealt with separately. First is shown the percentage of establishments of at least 50 employees where a closed shop covers at least a part of the workforce; for manual workers, closed shops occur in 29 per cent and for non-manuals in 6 per cent of establishments. The second row gives the proportion of all employees (in workforce of at least 50) who, on the managers' estimate, are actually members of closed shops in the different industries.

A part of the substantial variation between industries in the use of the closed shop may be accounted for by the relationship, shown in Table 4.2, between establishment size and the probability of a closed shop's being present. For both manuals and non-manuals the probability increases strongly with workforce size. If, however, we take into account the different proportions of establishment workforces that they constitute, then it is evident that the propensity for a non-manual closed shop to occur has a weaker relationship with total establishment size when compared with manual closed shops than was the case with the other indicators of union activity given in Table 4.2. Non-manual employees, it may be deduced, are in greater contrast with their manual counterparts when it comes to the closed shop than in other aspects of organisation.

As was the case with union membership density, the closed shop tends

TABLE 4.3

THE CLOSED SHOP BY INDUSTRY

(Percentages)

	All Manufac- turing	Food, Drink, Tobacco	Chemicals etc.	Metal Manufac- turing	Mechanical Engineering and Ships	Instrument, and Electrical Engineering	Vehicles	Metal Goods N.E.S.	Textiles	Clothing, Leather, Footwear	Bricks, Timber and Misc.	Paper, Printing and Pub- lishing
Manual												
Establishments with at least partial closed shop	29.5	66	36	29	25	10	25	23	20	16	17	68
Employees who are members of a closed shop	45.6	55	55	44	56	24	67	31	25	25	34	76
Non-Manual												
Establishments with at least partial closed shop	6.1	16	2	2	7	3	10	3	2	–	4	18
Employees who are members of a closed shop	9.8	10	3	1	8	4	21	8	4	2	9	29

to be a more total phenomenon within the workplace for manual than for non-manual employees. The closed shop covers over 90 per cent of manual employees in 83 per cent of establishments where a manual closed shop exists; for non-manuals the comparable figure is 53 per cent.

Aware that management may sometimes play a key part in administering a closed shop, we asked: 'Is this practice [union membership being a necessity for keeping a job] supported by an arrangement or agreement with management?' We distinguished between those that were 'open' and those that were 'tacit', and also those that had no management support at all.

For three-quarters of closed shops, management not only supported the practice by an arrangment or agreement but reported themselves to do so 'openly'. The proportion reporting open support for manual closed shops (non-manual in brackets) is 73 per cent (78 per cent), as against tacit support in 24 per cent (12 per cent) of cases, and no supportive arrangement or agreement in only 2 per cent (7 per cent) of closed shops. Expressed another way, 72 per cent of manual and 65 per cent of non-manual employees who are in closed shops are covered by open arrangements with management. The establishments reporting no managerial supportive arrangement at all are, for both manuals and non-manuals, almost exclusively in the printing industry where it is likely that long traditions of unilateral control through the chapels render management support irrelevant. Otherwise there is little variation in the pattern of support by industry, which may be partly a consequence of the fact that it does not appear to vary systematically with establishment size. Similarly, whether or not the establishment was foreign-owned made no difference; on the closed shop it appears that overseas companies differ little from the natives.

Clearly the closed shop is massively supported by management. Previous research has demonstrated that mangement's formal acknowledgment of a closed shop is often part and parcel of the formalisation of workplace bargaining (Department of Employment, 1971: 43). The study of the repealed Industrial Relations Act by Weekes, Mellish, Dickens and Lloyd (1975) demonstrated widespread connivance by management in preserving the closed shop in the face of legislation against it. We tested whether there were any signs that the Act had retarded the closed shop's development. The informal nature of the traditional closed shop made it impractical to ask a direct question about its age, but in those establishments where management had an agreement or arrangement of support we could ask how long that had been in effect. The average time stated was ten years for manual closed shops (seven years for non-manuals) and a very high proportion had come into being more recently. In the two years 1976 and 1977, 28 per cent (32 per cent) of existing closed shops had received management support, in 1974 and 1975, 11 per cent (8 per cent), and in the two years in which the Industrial Relations Act most clearly held sway, 1972 and 1973, 4 per cent (9 per cent). Since the figure for the preceding two years is 7 per cent (2 per cent), it is evident that the restraining effect of the Industrial Relations Act on management was slight but that the stimulus given by the Trade Union and Labour Relations Act of 1974 and 1975 may have been substantial.

Management involvement in the operation of the closed shop with the degree of formality implied in our question appears to be a comparatively recent phenomenon. Only 29 per cent of supportive arrangements for both manuals and non-manuals predate 1966 and, as has been noted, half of all arrangements and agreements have arisen since the beginning of 1970. There are marked variations between industries, with older closed shop arrangements in steel, heavy engineering, and printing. The youth of the widespread arrangements in food, drink and tobacco is particularly notable.

How reluctant has management been to provide this degree of support? We asked what advantages and what disadvantages, if any, the practice had for management and left the answers to be open-ended. The proportion reporting only advantages was 35 per cent for manuals (35 per cent for non-manuals) in contrast to only 14 per cent (4 per cent) who saw only disadvantages. A further 37 per cent (45 per cent) saw a bit of both. There can be no doubting the balance of advantage. Further inspection of the figures reveals that managers are more likely to see only advantages in industries where (with the exception of printing) the closed shop has been longer established. Familiarity with the closed shop appears to breed respect, or at least acquiescence.

The most common advantage cited was that the closed shop ensures that unions and stewards represent all employees (40 per cent of manual and 27 per cent of non-manual cases). This was followed by the view that the arrangement stabilises relationships between management and employees (21 per cent and 45 per cent) and that it ensures that procedures cover all employees (14 per cent and 10 per cent). The closed shop, in short, is seen as a procedural device that increases the representativeness and stability of collective bargaining.

The increased strength that the closed shop gives to unions was seen by managers as its greatest disadvantage (13 per cent and 22 per cent of those reporting disadvantages). Next came the view that it may restrict recruiting (11 per cent and 13 per cent) and that it makes for inflexibility in dealing with individuals and individual situations (13 per cent and 7 per cent). The criticism most often expressed in public debate, that individual freedom suffers under the closed shop, received less support (9 per cent and 7 per cent of those seeing disadvantages). Managers would appear to view the closed shop very pragmatically.

There can be little doubt that the character of the closed shop is changing. The spread of union membership agreements, especially in industries where there has been little previous experience of the closed shop, is involving management in its administration with a degree of formality that would often have been unthinkable only a decade ago. Furthermore, our survey suggested a clear tendency for more recently concluded closed shops to be more single-union that they were in the past. The closed shop as a reflection of workplace solidarity may be increasingly being replaced by an institution which is seen by management and the wider union primarily as an instrument of procedural discipline.

Multi-Unionism

The fact that there may be more than one trade union in a factory raises particular problems for workplace industrial relations. It is difficult to achieve and maintain collective agreements when the union side is divided in decision-making. Our survey asked which were the principal unions that management recognised and whether it dealt with them jointly or separately. We also asked about inter-union problems that had arisen during 1976 and 1977.

Only one manual union was recognised in 52 per cent of all establishments recognising manual unions (for non-manuals the figure is 64 per cent), and three or more were recognised in 22 per cent (14 per cent). But since, as Table 4.2 makes clear, the probability of more than one union being present increased sharply with the size of the workforce, multi-unionism was the experience of the majority of employees in manufacturing. Table 4.4 shows how the incidence of multi-unionism (expressed as a percentage of all establishments) varied across industries. The multi-union problems of large establishments are so well-known that it is a useful corrective to note that the majority of unionised plants in food, textiles, clothing, and many miscellaneous small industries had only one union for manual and one for non-manual employees. The recent growth of single union membership agreements just noted has undoubtedly played an important part in this.

Management negotiated with all manual unions together in 44 per cent of establishments where more than one was recognised. For non-manual unions these joint negotiating arrangements were rarer — they

TABLE 4.4

MULTI-UNIONISM BY INDUSTRY

(Percentages)

	All Manufacturing	Food, Drink, Tobacco	Chemicals etc.	Metal Manufacturing	Mechanical Engineering and Ships	Instrument, and Electrical Engineering	Vehicles	Metal Goods N.E.S.	Textiles	Clothing Leather, Footwear	Bricks, Timber and Misc.	Paper, Printing and Publishing
Manual												
Establishments with more than one union recognised	36.3	35	50	46	35	33	46	28	24	8	34	80
% of those with more than one union — Unions negotiate jointly	44.1	42	45	53	62	63	58	33	26	20	50	27
Inter-union problems have occurred	28.9	13	25	45	26	24	19	13	33	–	28	48
Non-Manual												
Establishments with more than one union recognised	13.1	6	11	19	21	24	34	10	5	1	9	14
Manual and Non-Manual												
'Work fairly closely together' where both are recognised	54.1	58	48	50	56	51	56	49	38	66	53	65

were only reported for 18 per cent of possible cases. In another 5 per cent of the manual cases there were sometimes occasions for joint negotiations and for a further 8 per cent some unions were dealt with jointly but others separately, typically where there was a strong craft tradition. The unions most consistent in negotiating alone were, unsurprisingly, those in the printing industry. The propensity to negotiate jointly shows no consistent variation with the size of the workforce, but it is, significantly, strongly associated with the presence of a full-time shop steward. Where there is a full-time steward in a multi-union establishment the chance of there being joint union negotiating arrangements was, allowing for workforce size, half as great again. Two mutually consistent implications are, first, that full-time stewards perform an integrating function and, second, that managements who cultivate joint union activity also encourage full-time shop stewards.

In the two years previous to the survey, managers reported that inter-union problems had occurred in 29 per cent of establishments with more than one recognised manual union (23 per cent of non-manuals). Such problems were more common in the larger establishments, especially those with more than a thousand employees. Over a quarter of the problems reported were concerned with demarcation between unions, particularly evident for both manual and non-manuals in the printing industry and also where Boilermakers were prominent. The second most common source of problems between manual unions (and third between non-manuals) was arguments over pay differentials, spread across most of industry. Although arguments over pay differentials are common enough within unions, it is likely that they are harder to resolve when between unions. Third for manuals (and first for non-manuals) were problems arising from recruitment and arguments over union membership; among the non-manuals A.S.T.M.S. and A.C.T.S.S. featured particularly prominently.

For most bargaining purposes manual and non-manual unions are segregated into strictly separate procedures and have little formal contact at the workplace. When asked about this, managers from only 3 per cent of establishments with both sorts of unions recognised said that they had 'poor relations with each other'. Another 38 per cent said that they had 'little to do with each other'. But the remaining 54 per cent reported that manual and non-manual unions in their establishment 'work fairly closely together'. As Table 4.4 demonstrates, this shows little variation between industries, neither does it vary systematically with establishment size.

Shop Steward Organisation

Shop stewards are almost as widespread as union recognition. Managers were asked whether their establishments had shop stewards or union representatives apart from health and safety representatives; their response suggested that stewards existed in 73 per cent of cases for manual workers and 34 per cent for non-manual. The industrial distribution of the extent of stewards is given in Table 4.1. Unsurprisingly, as Table 4.2 demonstrates, the probability of stewards' being found increases sharply with the size of the workforce. Stewards are an almost unvarying accompaniment to single-employer bargaining, whether at establishment or corporate level.

The replies imply that there are some 119,000 manual and 37,000 non-manual shop stewards in manufacturing establishments of 50 or more employees. They indicate that the average manual steward has a constituency of 31 union members and his non-manual counterpart one of 22 members. These estimates give substantially smaller constituencies (and thus more stewards) than earlier estimates drawing on union sources and suggest (as did the survey of management carried out by the Commission on Industrial Relations (1973)) that managers overestimate the number of stewards in their establishment.

In most establishments where there are stewards there is a degree of hierarchy. Asked whether any of the stewards at their workplace were 'acknowledged by management as senior representatives or conveners', those interviewed disclosed that such a post existed in 74 per cent of establishments where there were manual stewards and 61 per cent where there were non-manual stewards. Variation by industry is shown in Table 4.5 and by workforce size in Table 4.6. There is no unequivocal way of discounting for the size effect, but if we consider the industrial incidence of senior stewards separately for establishments with fewer than and with more than 500 employees, the variation declines substantially for both manuals and non-manuals. This is consistent with the argument of Brown, Ebsworth and Terry (1978) that the emergence of the senior steward is primarily a response to the size of the workforce and more particularly, to the size of the establishment's shop steward body.

A similar effect is evident when we look at the holding of regular shop steward meetings, a simple indicator of the routine nature of steward activity. Aware that managers' impressions of such things might be indistinct, we asked whether stewards or representatives held meetings 'amongst themselves with no other participants', regularly, occasionally, or never. In those establishments with stewards, the proportion of manual stewards holding meetings 'regularly' (with non-manual figures in brackets) was 37 per cent (30 per cent); meetings were reported 'occasionally' in

38 per cent (38 per cent), and 'never' in 22 per cent (27 per cent). With the exception of an unusually high propensity of manual stewards in the food industries to hold meetings regularly, and the reverse for both manuals and non-manuals in clothing and footwear, most of the inter-industry variation in Table 4.5 appears to be accounted for by the workforce size variation shown in Table 4.6. Allowing for the fact that non-manuals are a smaller proportion of the workforce than manuals, their respective sensitivities to size with regard to the institution of senior stewards and regular meetings are very similar.

The workforce size explanation is weaker when we turn to the phenom-enon of the full-time shop steward because there was a greater variation of response around the average figures given in Table 4.6. The proliferation of this job has been one of the most important developments of post-war British industrial relations. We asked managers whether any stewards in their establishment 'consistently spend more or less all their time, in practice, on workplace union affairs', adding the note that this applied only to employees paid by the company and not to full-time officials paid by the union. From their replies it appears that in 12 per cent of establishments with manual stewards at least one is full-time and in 2 per cent of establishments with non-manual stewards at least one is full-time. Table 4.5 shows a very uneven distribution of these individuals between industries, a variation which can be explained only in part by the tendency for them to be concentrated where the workforces are very large.

Full-time stewards were considerably more common, allowing for workforce size, where wages were fixed by single- rather than by multi-employer bargaining. This was true for both manual and non-manual full-time stewards, and suggests that the change in bargaining structure discussed in Chapter 2 has encouraged their emergence. In the previous chapter it was reported that, allowing for size effects, full-time stewards were correlated with the presence of a specialist industrial relations director. Other research in progress shows that, for a given establishment size, the probability of there being a full-time shop steward is substantially greater when the establishment is part of a large enterprise than when part of a small one, a finding that may reflect the greater specialisation of industrial relations management in larger enterprises. This is consistent with the argument of Brown, Ebsworth and Terry (1978) that full-time stewards have to a large extent come into being through managerial initiative.

In answer to our question as to how long there had been full-time stewards, the reply for both manuals and non-manuals was that in almost precisely half of all cases a position for a full-time steward had been created in the previous five years (that is, since the start of 1972). The

TABLE 4.5

SHOP STEWARD ORGANISATION BY INDUSTRY

(Expressed as a percentage of those establishments where a steward is present)

	All Manufacturing	Food, Drink, Tobacco	Chemicals etc.	Metal Manufacturing	Mechanical Engineering and Ships	Instrument, and Electrical Engineering	Vehicles	Metal Goods N.E.S.	Textiles	Clothing Leather Footwear	Bricks, Timber and Misc.	Paper, Printing and Publishing
Manual												
Recognised senior stewards	74.0	68	80	76	69	80	83	82	67	74	75	66
Full-time steward present	11.7	6	15	12	20	15	30	6	7	–	16	4
Regular steward meetings	36.8	61	49	29	36	35	58	38	30	10	37	29
Combine committee meetings (where not single establishment)	34.6	55	51	16	26	55	35	19	25	19	42	31
Where more than one union { cross representation	29.1	10	33	34	57	25	45	36	6	1	44	8
regular joint union meetings	52.2	14	49	66	94	82	42	43	23	–	56	32
Non-Manual[1]												
Recognised senior stewards	61.4	41	52	73	50	72	87	65	65	71	73	38
Full-time steward present	2.3	1	2	1	4	1	10	–	–	–	1	3
Regular steward meetings	30.0	28	46	43	39	25	43	28	24	7	24	16
Combine committee meetings (where not single establishment)	43.3	67	53	38	37	59	38	22	45	14	34	64

establishments where there had been full-time shop stewardships for longer periods were concentrated predominantly in vehicles, mechanical engineering, and steel and, to a lesser extent, in printing and chemicals. The industries most notable for the recent arrival of the post were textiles and clothing.

TABLE 4.6

SHOP STEWARD ORGANISATION BY WORKFORCE SIZE

(Expressed as a percentage of those establishments where a steward is present)

	Number of full-time employees				
	50–99	100–199	200–499	500–999	1000+
Manual					
Recognised senior stewards	66	68	81	91	97
Full-time steward present	3	3	13	32	70
Regular steward meetings	26	23	44	73	83
Combine committee meetings (where not single establishment)	25	29	37	46	65
Where more than one union { cross-representation	15	31	30	37	41
regular joint union meetings	21	43	61	57	68
Non-Manual					
Recognised senior stewards	48	37	67	77	88
Full-time steward present	–	–	1	2	13
Regular steward meetings	1	16	37	47	69
Combine committee meetings (where not single establishment)	49	39	34	44	63

We estimate from these replies that in 1978 there were some 3,500 full-time manual stewards in 1,800 manufacturing establishments, and some 300 full-time non-manual stewards in 160 manufacturing establishments. It is a fine matter for interpretation whether a steward is in fact fully involved in union duties when the majority of full-time stewards have token jobs (if only so that they have a constituency to elect them). Consequently this result is not seriously out of line with the estimate of Brown *et al.*'s (1978) 1976 survey of shop stewards that there were 'approximately 5000 full-time stewards covering manual workers in approximately 3000 manufacturing establishments'. Managers are less likely to admit to so heavy a commitment to union duties than the stewards themselves. Since the McCarthy and Parker (1968) survey for 1966, with which Brown *et al*. made comparison, was also using replies from stewards themselves, there is no reason to revise the conclusion that 'the number of full-time stewards in manufacturing industry has probably quadrupled over the decade' since 1966. It is in accord with the data on the growth of full-time shop-stewardships just reported.

TABLE 4.7

A COMPAR` 3ON OF THE PRESENT SURVEY WITH THE RESULTS ON SHOP
STEWARD ORGANISATION FROM THE 1976 STEWARD SURVEY

	Percentage of all establishments with shop steward which have:					
	Senior Steward		Full-time Steward		Regular Meetings	
Size of Workforce	1976 Steward Survey	1978 Manager Survey	1976 Steward Survey	1978 Manager Survey	1976 Steward Survey	1978 Manager Survey
100–249	65	69	10	4	48	26
250–499	84	81	31	15	74	46
500–999	96	91	54	32	83	73
1000–1999	97	96	60	65	90	81
2000+	100	100	73	83	89	88

Note: 1976 survey data in Brown, Ebsworth and Terry (1978).

Further light is cast by a closer comparison with Brown *et al*.'s 1976 survey which contained an unsystematic sample of 246 manufacturing establishments. Some of the 1978 questions were couched in the same terms. Table 4.7 gives the breakdown by workforce size of questions relating to senior stewards, full-time stewards and regular shop steward meetings. It is apparent that the findings for senior stewards are remarkably close; managerial definitions of seniority appear to tally closely with those of the stewards themselves. The reported awareness of regular shop steward meetings, however, is very different in all but the largest workplaces; managers appear to show little awareness of this aspect of their stewards' organisation except where, as is the case with shop steward bodies numbering some dozens, special facilities have to be made available for meetings. Perhaps the most interesting difference occurs with the figures for full-time shop stewards. The first point to note is that in establishments of under 1,000 employees the divergence between managerial and steward notions of being more or less 'full-time' are substantial, presumably because the role is less formalised than in the large establishments. Second, in the large establishments the estimates derived from management responses in 1978 suggest a greater incidence of full-timers than those derived from stewards themselves in 1976. The most likely explanation of this is that the rapid growth in the number of full-time shop stewards in manufacturing that was deduced to have occurred in the decade up to 1976 continued during the following two years.

Inter-Union Organisation

Multi-unionism may present a major problem for shop steward organisation if rivalries and differences in procedure of outside unions inhibit decision-making within the shop steward body. Two indicators of how far these problems have been overcome are the extent to which stewards 'represent workers belonging to other unions apart from their own', which we call 'cross-representation', and the extent to which shop steward meetings 'ever involve stewards from more than one union'. Comparison of different industries in these matters is far from straight-forward. In some circumstances trade union growth has occurred so as to separate unions so distinctly in different departments that the question of cross-representation never arises. Then again, in some production technologies unions are subject to such different working conditions, as where there are process and maintenance workers in chemical refineries, that regular joint-union steward activity might be of little value. Consequently an absence of these signs of inter-union co-operation is not necessarily a sign of weakness.

Cross-representation among manual unions was reported in 29 per cent of establishments having stewards and more than one union. For non-manuals it is reported in only 7 per cent. As Tables 4.5 and 4.6 show, it is, for manual workers, most evident in the heavy engineering and vehicles industries and shows little sensitivity to the size of the workforce. Cross-representation is also associated with the presence of full-time shop stewards and with joint trade union shop steward meetings.

The inclusion of more than one union in manual shop steward meetings is a 'regular' occurrence in 52 per cent of establishments which have stewards meetings and more than one union. It is an 'occasional' occurrence in a further 15 per cent. There is a clear link with managerial bargaining practice. Where management negotiates with manual unions jointly there is a three times larger likelihood of their having joint steward meetings and a four times larger likelihood of cross-representation than where negotiations are carried out separately.

Inter-Workplace Organisation

Almost three-quarters of manufacturing establishments of 50 or more employees (employing 84 per cent of employees) are not independent but are part of multi-establishment companies. Whether or not these comprise a single bargaining unit, they present a serious challenge for steward organisations. Having built up a capability for collective action *within* the establishment, stewards are confronted with the need to develop links between establishments if they are to prevent the common employer setting one against the other and under-mining their hard-won establishment effectiveness. Thus the growth of industrial concentration in Britain and the development of corporate bargaining has been accompanied by talk of 'combine committees'. Consequently our survey asked whether meetings took place between stewards or representatives from the interviewee's establishment and others working in other parts of the same organisation.

Managers reported themselves aware of some sort of manual combine committee activity in a third of all establishments which were part of multi-plant organisations and also had stewards. They reported it to be 'regular' in 13 per cent and 'occasional' in 21 per cent of places. Interestingly enough, it was more widespread among non-manual steward organisations: 'regular' meetings occurred in 15 per cent and 'occasional' meetings in 29 per cent of establishments.

The industrial distribution of combine committees (to lend a grand name to what is often a very informal and *ad hoc* occurrence) is given in Table 4.5, covering all such committees, whether or not they meet regularly. It is apparent that combine activity is most common in industries where it rarely finds the newspaper headlines: food, chemicals, instrument and electrical engineering, and the catch-all 'bricks, timber, and miscellaneous' category. For the non-manuals, paper and printing feature more prominently. This concentration outside the traditional heartlands of shop steward organisation is the more surprising given the fact that, as Table 4.6 shows, for manual workers the probability of combine activity increases substantially with workforce size.

The reason for this distribution becomes apparent when the level of pay bargaining is taken into account. Combine activity, and particularly regular combine activity, is very much less common where bargaining occurs at establishment rather than at corporate or industry level. For manual workers, combines were evident in 52 per cent of cases where there was group or divisional bargaining, as compared with 38 per cent where multi-employer industry agreements prevailed and only 29 per cent where the most important level of bargaining was the establishment itself. This relationship between bargaining level and the occurrence of combines still held when we considered the sample in five separate categories of workforce size. Non-manual combines were more common where there were multi-employer industry agreements than corporate ones (63 per cent compared to 55 per cent of cases) but both out-numbered the establishment-level cases (36 per cent) and did so even more substantially for regular combines.

The propensity for stewards to form links between establishments within multi-plant companies clearly depends to a considerable extent upon the employers' choice of pay bargaining level. Where stewards are brought together from different establishments in a company for a corporate negotiation, the combine is to a large extent management sponsored. Management makes the arrangements and pays for the travel. More surprising at first sight is the common occurrence, particularly for non-manual workers, of combines in association with multi-employer industry agreements. Here the very weakness of the domestic steward organisation, evidenced by the continuing importance of multi-employer agreements, may provide the explanation. Steward organisations with traditions of strong and independent workplace bargaining are inhibited from forming effective coalitions with stewards in other establishments in the same company. It is where an establishment's steward organisation has less capacity to act independently — as with non-manuals and where multi-employer agreements still hold sway — that combine committee co-operation is easier to sustain.

Relations with the Outside Union

There is no simple way, least of all through the eyes of managers, of assessing the extent to which shop steward organisations are dependent upon the outside union officialdom. Previous studies have shown there to be a complex and generally very co-operative relationship between stewards and full-time union officials; the officials tend to concentrate their energies where steward organisation is weak but maintain good contacts where it is strong (Boraston, Clegg and Rimmer, 1975). We probed this by asking 'from the point of view of management, how important are external trade union officers from manual (non-manual) unions to industrial relations here?', and we defined 'importance' in terms of the extent to which they 'take the lead'.

It was reported that outside officials *always* took the lead from manual stewards in 16 per cent of establishments where there were manual stewards. This occurred less frequently for the non-manuals: in 9 per

TABLE 4.8(a)

RELATIONSHIPS WITH MANAGEMENT AND FULL-TIME OFFICIALS, CHECK-OFF, AND INCREASED FORMALISATION

	All Manufacturing	Food, Drink, Tobacco	Chemicals etc.	Metal Manufacturing
Manual				
Regular meetings with management[a]	39.2	43	51	50
Full-time trade union officials felt to be important[a]	56.3	63	51	44
Check-off of dues operated[b]	57.7	93	96	71
Non-Manual				
Regular meetings with management[a]	29.6	25	30	43
Full-time trade union officials felt to be important[a]	52.6	77	40	35
Check-off of dues operated[b]	56.6	80	87	66
Both Manual and Non-Manual				
Management relations with stewards more formal in last five years[a]	47.1	58	49	46

(a) expressed as a percentage of establishments where stewards are present

(b) expressed as a percentage of establishments where unions are recognised

cent of establishments which had non-manual stewards. They *sometimes* took the lead (and were thus classed as 'fairly' important) in 40 per cent of manual and 43 per cent of non-manual cases. Outside officials were said to 'rarely play an important part' in 28 per cent of manual (28 per cent non-manual) cases, and to be not at all important in 13 per cent (19 per cent). The typical picture of managers' perceptions of the role of the full-time official might thus be summarised by saying that the official assists rather than dominates the steward.

The variations in this role between industries are shown in Table 4.8 for cases where the full-time official was felt to be 'very' or 'fairly' important. For manual workers, he is more important outside the engineering and chemicals industries. For non-manuals the full-time officials play an exceptionally prominent role in food, drink, and tobacco, and in paper and printing. It will be noticed that there is a marked size effect, with the

TABLE 4.8(a) *continued*

INDUSTRY							
Mechanical Engineering and Ships	Instrument and Electrical Engineering	Vehicles	Metal Goods N.E.S.	Textiles	Clothing, Leather, Footwear	Bricks, Timber and Misc.	Paper, Printing and Publishing
59	37	49	36	47	12	38	21
51	46	36	52	60	53	65	76
26	42	41	42	68	70	58	49
32	24	26	13	(30)	(15)	41	34
57	61	33	45	(46)	(37)	38	85
34	44	64	41	(76)	(81)	57	56
46	68	48	54	51	31	46	30

officials being more involved in the larger establishments, but the industrial variations just noted hold even when account is taken of this. Once again, as Boraston, Clegg and Rimmer argued, it is the structure of bargaining which appears to play a key part. A prominent role for outside officials is associated more with multi-employer than with single-employer wage bargaining. For both manual and non-manual workers, full-time officials take the lead substantially more often where there are industry-wide multi-employer agreements than where there are single-establishment or corporate agreements.

Relations with Management and the Use of Check-off Arrangements

The existence of a shop steward organisation does not of itself tell us anything about the extent of the recognition it receives from management. It is quite possible for stewards to deal solely with first-line supervision

TABLE 4.8(b)
RELATIONSHIPS WITH MANAGEMENT AND FULL-TIME OFFICIALS,
CHECK-OFF, AND INCREASED FORMALISATION

	NUMBER OF EMPLOYEES				
	50–99	100–199	200–499	500–999	1000+
Manual					
Regular meetings with management[a]	29	31	46	65	72
Full-time trade union officials felt to be important[a]	44	53	69	65	71
Check-off of dues operated[b]	46	55	65	75	79
Non-Manual					
Regular meetings with management[a]	(23)	12	31	39	51
Full-time trade union officials felt to be important[a]	(64)	29	52	54	61
Check-off of dues operated[b]	(43)	51	54	72	83
Both Manual and Non-Manual					
Management relations with stewards more formal in last 5 years[a]	41	38	57	63	61

(a) expressed as a percentage of establishments where stewards are present
(b) expressed as a percentage of establishments where unions are recognised

and never get access to higher management. We therefore asked 'how often does management above foreman level meet manual (non-manual) stewards or representatives to discuss workplace industrial relations?' and distinguished between such meetings being regular and irregular as a clue to how routine they were.

Some sort of meeting with management above foreman level occurs at least once a month for two-thirds of manual steward organisations and for half of non-manual. Such meetings are 'regular' for 39 per cent of manual and 30 per cent of non-manual cases, and they 'never' occurred in, respectively, 2 per cent and 4 per cent. It is thus normal for stewards to have regular access beyond their foremen. How this varies by industry and size is shown in Table 4.8. The size effect is strong and accounts for much of the inter-industry variation. Regular meetings with manual stewards are particularly associated with single-employer pay bargaining, whether corporate or establishment.

A particularly strong support that management can give to a domestic union organisation is to collect its union dues for it: variously called 'deduction at source' and 'check-off'. We asked whether this was operated and, if so, for how long. It emerges that the check-off is used for manual unions in 58 per cent of establishments where they are recognised and for non-manual unions in an almost identical 57 per cent. As Table 4.8 shows, use of check-off increases markedly with workforce size, so that the percentage of trade union members covered in 1978 was a massive 73 per cent for manual and 72 per cent for non-manual manufacturing employees. Its use is particularly associated with the general unions TGWU, GMWU, and USDAW and has progressed least far in the engineering industries where it was opposed by the AUEW until quite recently.

The widespread use of the check-off is remarkable in itself, but more remarkable is the newness of its arrival. The great bulk of check-off arrangements had come into being in the decade preceding our survey: 93 per cent for manuals and 92 per cent for non-manuals. Most dated from the five years since 1972: 65 per cent of manuals and 80 per cent of non-manuals. The spread of check-off for manual workers over the period since 1972 has been at a fairly even pace; for non-manuals it had gathered pace, with 44 per cent of arrangements having been established in the years 1976 and 1977. The youngest check-off arrangements are in the engineering industries where the practice still has some way to go.

The collection of union dues is not a topic that most people would think capable of drama, but the implications of this surge of check-off arrangements make it one of the key features in the changing pattern of British industrial relations. The role of the shop steward as collector of union dues (and thus what was often an important source of contact with the members) is all but gone, and with it the full-time official's hitherto perennial worries about embezzlement and falling out of membership. Perhaps most important is the way in which the check-off shifts the burden of administering the closed shop more than ever to management. For 72 per cent of manual closed shops (69 per cent of non-manual) there is a check-off arrangement in being. The recent growth of check-off arrangements must rank as one of the most important advances in union security in the history of British trade unionism.

The introduction of check-off is about as specific an institutional change as one can wish for, but we tried to detect more diffuse change in the relationship between managements and their domestic union organisations by asking 'in general are there any ways in which management has put its relationship with shop stewards or representatives on a more formal basis in the last 5 years?' and what form, if any, they took.

Almost half, 47 per cent, the establishments reported a formalising of relations with stewards since 1972. As Table 4.8 shows, the incidence of the change varies between industries and increases with workforce size. It is particularly strongly associated with multi-plant as opposed to single establishment companies, with the presence of a full-time shop steward, and with single-employer as opposed to multi-employer bargaining. More formal manager-steward relations are reported from 54 per cent of places for which the dominant level of manual pay bargaining is corporate or establishment, compared with 40 per cent of those with some multi-employer arrangement.

Asked to describe the nature of the change, managers named three main forms, each of which accounted for about a quarter of those reporting change. These were the introduction of regular meetings with stewards, the introduction of recognised stewards, and the formalising of arrangements between management and stewards. About one in seven mentioned that unions had been recognised for the first time (notably from smaller establishments) and that recognition had been extended to new groups. Other responses referred more loosely to more communication, greater consultation or the introduction of new procedures. Changes such as these do not come singly, and perhaps the simplest summary is that in the five years after 1972 almost half the manufacturing establishments of 50 or more employees took tangible steps to strengthen and formalise the position of their shop stewards.

Non-Union Representatives

This chapter has concerned itself so far with trade union activity because it is the basis of collective bargaining. But workplace industrial relations can involve other patterns of representation. A fascinating figure on the fringe of trade union activity is the non-union representative, perceived as a spokesman for his work-mates by management and possible himself a union member but not, for one reason or another, working through union channels, however unofficial. The Commission on Industrial Relations study of 1971 had detected large numbers of these people. We narrowed down our definition to exclude the Health and Safety representatives required by recent legislation.

Non-union employee representatives were reported from over a quarter of manufacturing establishments of 50 or more employees. They were in existence for both manual and non-manual employees at 14 per cent of establishments, for just manual at 4 per cent, and for just non-manual at 8 per cent. Of the establishments reporting them, almost half had no recognised unions, but the remainder reported not only recognised unions but shop stewards and even, in some cases, full-time shop stewards. It will be evident from Table 4.9 that for manual, but not for non-manual, employees, the incidence of non-union representatives diminishes with workforce size.

Health and Safety Committees

The Health and Safety at Work Act of 1974 stated that employers would eventually have to provide for the appointment of employee safety representatives and, subsequently, if requested, a safety committee with employee representatives. We enquired whether establishments had 'a joint management and employee *committee* set up just to deal with Health and Safety matters' and, if so, whether it was 'introduced after the publication of the Health and Safety at Work Bill in 1974'.

Health and Safety Committees were reported from 69 per cent of manufacturing establishments. Of these, 59 per cent had been established after the Bill and might be considered to have been inspired by the demonstrative effect of that Bill. It is apparent from Table 4.9 that the textile and clothing industries are most obviously lagging behind others in introducing these committees and that they are (unsurprisingly) longest established in the chemicals and metal manufacturing industries. The incidence of Health and Safety Committees is the greater the larger the establishment, but they tend to be more recent where workforces are smaller. Committees are least likely to exist where trade unions are not recognised. On the face of it, at least in formal terms, the legislation has had a very substantial impact.

Joint Consultation

Finally, we examine the practice often seen as being in conflict with collective bargaining: joint consultation. When McCarthy surveyed the fate of joint consultative committees established in the 1940s he concluded that 'either they must change their character and become essentially negotiating committees carrying out functions which are indistinguishable from the formal processes of shop floor bargaining, or they are boycotted by shop stewards and, as the influence of the latter grow, fall into disuse' (McCarthy, 1967; 33). We asked 'do you have any other joint committees of managers and employees here [i.e. besides health and safety committees] which are primarily concerned with *consultation* rather than

TABLE 4.9(a)

REPRESENTATIVE ACTIVITY OUTSIDE TRADE UNION CHANNELS

	All Manufacturing	Food, Drink, Tobacco	Chemicals etc.	Metal Manufacturing
Joint Consultative Committee exists	42.4	39	55	48
% of J.C.C.s introduced in last five years	60.7	71	42	29
% of J.C.Cs. for which all reps. come through union	30.1	18	26	52
Health and Safety Committee exists	69.5	82	84	77
% of H&S Committees set up after H&S Bill (1974)	58.6	75	43	32
Manual *non-union* representative present	18.8	3	26	10
Non-manual *non-union* representative present	22.3	9	49	15

negotiation?' and, if so, 'have these been introduced within the last five years?', the latter being partly to detect any indication of whether the mid-1970s enthusiasm for what might be summarily called industrial democracy had had any effect. To discern whether such committees were wholly integrated into the steward organisation, we asked 'are the employee representatives chosen through trade union channels?'. Finally, 'from a management point of view, would you say the operation of the committee(s) is very/usually/occasionally/not very successful?'

Joint consultative committees were reported from 42 per cent of establishments, with their incidence, as Table 4.9 shows, increasing sharply with workforce size. The majority of them, 61 per cent, had been introduced since 1972. Although they were slightly more common where there was single-employer bargaining over manual wages, and where shop stewards were well-established, there is no obvious explanation of the variation in industrial distribution.

The employee representatives were exclusively appointed to joint consultative committees through union channels in only 30 per cent of cases, although some came that way in another 13 per cent. Thus, over

TABLE 4.9(a) *continued*

| | INDUSTRY | | | | | | |
Mechanical Engineering and Ships	Instrument and Electrical Engineering	Vehicles	Metal Goods N.E.S.	Textiles	Clothing, Leather, Footwear	Bricks, Timber and Misc.	Paper, Printing and Pub-lishing
33	40	68	50	58	18	42	40
53	71	81	50	87	79	48	53
56	32	42	13	11	8	30	45
77	68	76	72	52	53	69	64
62	69	57	66	54	85	44	45
16	14	25	18	44	14	27	7
14	19	40	22	46	13	23	17

half were not automatically a part of the collective bargaining process. It will be seen from Table 4.9, however, that trade union domination of the committees increases with workforce size so as to monopolise employee representation in over half of the joint consultative committees in work-places of 500 or more employees. Where a full-time manual steward is present, trade union channels are used for appointing all representatives on 64 per cent of consultative committees.

Managers showed a cheerful view of their committees' success. Over two-thirds considered them to be at least usually successful; 27 per cent said 'very', 43 per cent 'usually', 24 per cent 'occasionally', and a trivial 4 per cent 'not very' successful. Enthusiasm was markedly less in establish-ments with a strike record, and also, interestingly, where the committees had been established since 1972: managers reported success at least 'usually' with 81 per cent of committees established before 1972 while the more recent arrivals gained only 65 per cent comparable approval. It may be that success in joint consultation comes slowly. Perhaps recent moves on consultation had included hasty and cosmetic attempts to adjust to the spirit of the Bullock Committee.

TABLE 4.9(b)

REPRESENTATIVE ACTIVITY OUTSIDE TRADE UNION CHANNELS

	NUMBER OF EMPLOYEES				
	50–99	100–199	200–499	500–999	1000+
Joint Consultative Committee exists	29	42	56	62	77
% of J.C.Cs. introduced in last 5 years	70	53	60	61	54
% of J.C.Cs. for which all reps. come through union	35	34	34	57	57
Health and Safety Committee exists	57	70	86	82	90
% of H&S Committees set up after H&S Bill (1974)	70	66	47	41	34
Manual *non-union* representative present	23	17	16	14	5
Non-manual *non-union* representative present	21	19	27	25	23

Whatever the cause of the resurgence of joint consultation, it is difficult to avoid the conclusion that McCarthy's findings have to be modified. His research related to a time when shop stewards had little option but either to take over or to bury consultative arrangements because there were few formal channels for workplace negotiation. This lack has largely been remedied and the degree of recognition now afforded to shop stewards is unlikely to be threatened by the introduction of consultation.

Conclusion

It is hard to overstate the significance of the change that workplace trade union organisation has undergone in the last decade. The authoritative picture drawn by McCarthy and Parker in 1968 was indeed of active shop steward organisations, but the authors stressed their variability between establishments, their close but informal relations with management, and their resourcefulness in operating despite external multi-employer agreements.

The present survey reveals considerable similarity between industries in the state of steward organisatons, once the effect of workforce size is allowed for; there is still variability, but it has diminished substantially since the 1960s. Moreover, non-manual employees have steward organisations which are, at least on the indicators we have used, almost as developed as those of their manual workmates. The spread of steward organisations to industries where they were hitherto unusual has been accompanied by a marked increase in the formality of the stewards' position, most clearly exemplified by the doubling and redoubling in the number of full-time stewards over the decade.

Shop stewards are no longer divorced from formal negotiating arrangements in the way that the Donovan Commission had criticised. The formal arrangements have in the main been adapted to include them and the concomitant rise of single-employer bargaining has increasingly made stewards into the principal negotiators and guarantors of clear-cut factory agreements and procedures.

It seems likely that the nature of trade unionism has undergone a fundamental change. Throughout manufacturing, but particularly where steward organisations have arisen 'ready-made', management has had a powerful influence in shaping what was previously largely independent. The rapid spread of closed shop agreements, check-off arrangements, full-time stewards, and consultative committees all tell of a management involvement in workplace union administration which was unthinkable a decade ago.

5

Strikes and Other Industrial Action

Strikes are unavoidably of central concern in industrial relations. The official statistics, however, frequently have their accuracy challenged and they completely ignore other forms of industrial action. Our survey gave us an opportunity to gain a fuller picture of the incidence of collective sanctions, to relate them to a wide range of other characteristics, and to test official measures.

Respondents were asked 'which, if any, of these forms of industrial action have actually taken place here in the last two years'. They were then given a list of six forms of action and asked to specify which had occurred, taking manual and non-manual workers separately. The results are directly comparable only to those of the surveys of *Workplace Industrial Relations* carried out in 1972 and 1973 (Parker, 1974; 1975). The survey of 1968 asked about action experienced by respondents since they had been in their present posts (Government Social Survey, 1968) and the more recent study by Daniel (1976) asked about action in the previous twelve months, not two years. It is thus difficult to assess how far the results of the present survey suggest any marked changes in the level of industrial action. We can, however, compare the distribution of action between strikes, overtime bans, and other forms with all these earlier surveys. The only type of action previously surveyed that we omitted was the category 'threats to strike'. The pilot survey revealed that this definitionally difficult concept was of little value since, as several respondents put it, 'they're always threatening to strike'.

The present survey went further than its predecessors in two important directions. First, respondents were asked to estimate the *number of times* a given sanction had been used in the previous two years. From this evidence it is possible to estimate the 'proneness to industrial action' of various types of establishment. In addition to giving the *proportion of establishments* of a given size which experienced industrial action, it is possible to calculate the *number of incidents of action per employee* in such establishments. These two distinct forms of analysis will be used in the following sections.

80

The second innovation was to ask respondents who had had a strike lasting at least one whole day or shift for details of this strike. The requested information included the length of the strike and the numbers of strikers and workers laid off as a result. This evidence is of interest in itself, but it also enabled us to make estimates of the number of strikes qualifying for the Department of Employment's strike statistics. This is the first time that such a direct estimate of the coverage of the Department's statistics has been made.

The Distribution of Industrial Action

Forms of Action

The use of each form of industrial action by manual and non-manual workers is shown in the weighted data given in Table 5.1. Nearly 46 per cent of establishments reported some form of action by manual workers; 9 per cent reported such action by non-manual employees. One-third of establishments had experienced a strike by manual workers; for non-manual workers the proportion was one in twenty. Industrial action

TABLE 5.1

FORMS OF INDUSTRIAL ACTION BY MANUAL AND NON-MANUAL WORKERS

	Per cent of establishments reporting action		Per cent distribution of individual incidents of action	
	Manual	Non-manual	Manual	Non-manual
Strikes less than 1 day	20.1	1.8	26.5	15.9
Strike one day or more	20.8	4.1	16.5	23.5
Overtime ban	22.8	4.4	26.5	27.3
Work to rule	12.2	3.4	12.7	23.5
Go slow	4.4	0.6	13.3	3.3
Work in	2.2	0.8	1.5	3.5
Other	3.4	0.3	3.0	3.2
Any strike	32.8	5.3	43.0	39.4
Any other action	28.7	5.8	57.0	60.5
Any action	45.7	9.4		
No action	54.3	90.6		
TOTAL	100.0	100.0	100.0	100.0

short of a strike was almost as popular: such action by manual workers was reported in 29 per cent of establishments. Of the individual forms of action listed, the overtime ban affected two-thirds the number of establishments affected by strikes. The work to rule was the only other type of action which affected a substantial number of plants.

The table also shows the relative frequency of each type of action. Thus, of all the manual actions reported, 43 per cent were strikes. These findings on relative frequency are generally in accord with those on the proportion of establishments affected in the picture they give of the relative popularity of different forms of action.

Data on the number of incidents of action may be broken down to show the number of establishments which had only one incident of any type, the number having two incidents, and so on. This is done in Table 5.2. Of the plants having any form of action, nearly half experienced only one incident. Very few plants had more than four non-manual incidents, whereas over 100 manual incidents were reported in some plants. As the distribution of *incidents* of action shows, plants having a large number of incidents accounted for a large proportion of the total. Establishments reporting over 100 incidents by manual workers formed only 0.3 per cent of the total, but accounted for 17 per cent of all incidents of industrial action by such workers. These plants could reasonably be described as those where industrial action is 'endemic' (McCarthy, 1966).

TABLE 5.2

FREQUENCY DISTRIBUTION OF ALL INCIDENTS OF INDUSTRIAL ACTION OVER TWO-YEAR PERIOD

Establishments reporting:	% Establishments		% Incidents	
	Manual	Non-manual	Manual	Non-manual
1 incident	20.6	5.3	10.5	22.5
2 incidents	7.8	1.4	7.9	12.1
3 incidents	4.9	1.5	7.6	18.8
4 incidents	2.9	0.5	5.9	8.0
5–10 incidents	5.4	0.3	19.5	10.3
11–20 incidents	2.9	0.4	18.9	22.1
21–30 incidents	0.6	–	7.0	3.8
31–100 incidents	0.3	–	5.7	3.8
101–200 incidents	0.3	–	17.0	2.5
No incident	54.3	90.6		
TOTAL	100.0	100.0	100.0	100.0

Comparison with Previous Surveys

In 1972, 32 per cent of senior managers reported non-national strikes during the previous two years (Parker, 1974: 64). In 1975, 24 per cent of establishments reported strikes during the previous year (Daniel, 1976: 10). Thus, recalling our finding of 33 per cent during the previous two years, the incidence of strike action seems to have remained fairly stable. In the present survey, action other than strikes was reported in 29 per cent of establishments, however, as against 38 per cent in 1972. This difference may be partly due to the exclusion from the present survey of 'threats to strike' but, as Table 5.3 shows, this cannot be the whole explanation. In 1968 works managers and personnel managers had experienced more overtime bans than they had strikes. By 1972, overtime bans were reported in 24 per cent of establishments, compared with strikes in 32 per cent, a ratio of overtime bans to strikes of 75:100. By 1978, the ratio had fallen to 69:100. As Table 5.3 shows, similar trends occurred for other forms of action. It thus appears that the relative importance of action short of a strike has fallen.

TABLE 5.3

TRENDS IN INDUSTRIAL ACTION, 1968–78: NUMBER OF ESTABLISHMENTS EXPERIENCING GIVEN ACTION AS PERCENTAGE OF NUMBER EXPERIENCING STRIKES

	1968		*1972*	*1975*	*1978*
Strike	100	100	100	100	100
Overtime Ban	110	137	75	71	69
Work to Rule	60	77	59	64	37
Go Slow	60	66	28	29	13
Work In	na	na	na	12	7
Strike Threat	110	131	63	208	na
Other	na	na	22	10	10
Source:	(G.S.S., 1968)		(Parker, 1974)	(Daniel, 1975)	(IRRU)
Respondents:	Works Managers	Personnel Managers	Senior Managers	Managers	Senior Managers

Writing in 1965, Flanders noted that 'one of the notable features of workplace relations in recent years, not revealed by strike figures, has been the increasing use of "cut price" industrial action such as overtime bans, working to rule or going slow' (1970:112). Although Tables 5.1 and 5.3 show that such cut price action is still very popular, it appears, on the limited comparisons possible here, that its use has been declining during

TABLE 5.4

MANUAL INDUSTRIAL ACTION BY INDUSTRY

	% Establishments reporting			Incidents per 100,000 manual employees		Incidents per establishment		% incidents accounted for by	
	Any action	Any strikes	Any other action	All	All Strikes	All	All Strikes	Strikes under 1 day	Strikes over 1 day
Food, etc.	45.8	39.2	32.5	1360	869	3.0	1.9	46.6	17.2
Chemical, etc.	37.7	32.5	26.0	709	261	1.5	0.5	11.8	25.1
Metal manufac.	46.4	31.9	36.0	649	269	2.0	0.8	25.3	16.1
Mech. Eng. and Ships	45.6	30.2	31.1	653	374	1.9	0.7	19.1	18.9
Instrument and Electrical Eng.	47.1	32.6	33.8	615	248	1.4	0.6	20.9	19.4
Vehicles	71.1	65.3	48.4	869	433	4.4	2.2	33.3	16.6
Metal Goods N.E.S.	45.5	26.4	32.4	2520	415	3.6	0.6	9.2	7.3
Textiles	62.5	54.1	14.4	695	456	1.1	0.7	49.4	16.2
Clothing	31.0	28.8	5.3	548	435	0.7	0.6	50.8	28.6
Bricks, Timber and Misc.	39.4	23.4	28.4	1060	450	1.6	0.7	23.5	19.2
Printing, Paper and Publishing	43.0	16.6	38.9	1010	338	1.4	0.5	19.1	14.3
ALL	45.7	32.8	28.7	992	436	2.0	0.9	26.5	16.5

the 1970s. Many reasons could be suggested for this, and lengthy specula-
tion here would be pointless. However, two possibilities may be mentioned.
First, the increasing relative importance of the strike occurred at a time
when total strike activity (as measured by official statistics) was falling.
It is possible that the peak of strike activity in the early 1970s may have
been accompanied by a peak in the use of other forms of pressure.
Secondly, the subsequent decline in the relative importance of sanctions
other than strikes may be associated with a more defensive posture
taken by the union movement. Employers may be more prepared to hold
out against limited actions when they are operating at a low level of
capacity (and thus when overtime bans and the like are relatively painless)
than when they want to maximize production. Hence, strikes may become
relatively more powerful means of meeting workers' demands when
unemployment levels are higher.

Distribution by Industry
The occurrence and frequency of industrial action by manual workers in
eleven industry groups during the two years covered by the survey are
shown in Table 5.4. The percentage of establishments in each industry
that reported having had industrial action shows little variation. The
vehicles and, more surprisingly, the textiles industries are above average,
and clothing below. There is, however, considerably greater inter-industry
variation in both measures of frequency. When the size of the workforce
is taken into account the vehicles industry falls back to an average
position. On both frequency per 100,000 employees and frequency per
establishment the food, drink, and tobacco group of industries moves to
the fore.

None of these three measures is directly comparable with the Department of Employment's published statistics. A single, industry-wide strike,
for instance, would here appear as a separate incident in each establishment.
There are two points to be made about the comparison. The first is that
the official figures on strike rates, while showing the considerable variation
in the frequency of action between industry, obscure the more evenly
spread tendency to have experienced some action. The second point arises
from testing the correlation between the Department's data on the
number of strikes per head in 1976–77 and the figures in Table 5.4 for
the nine comparable industry groups. The correlation with our data for
incidents per establishment was quite strong (a coefficient of 0.75) but
there was no correlation at all with our measure of the number of incidents
per 100,000 employees. The latter measure would seem to be the less
useful indicator of frequency and we shall return to the question of its
interpretation later.

The final section of Table 5.4 shows how much the relative importance of different sorts of industrial action varies between industries. A considerable amount of the deviation between our measure of strike frequency and that of the Department of Employment's is explained by the fact that the Department's definition usually excludes strikes of less than a day or shift. Strikes tend to be shorter in some industries than in others. Furthermore, the use of strikes as against other forms of action varies substantially between industries: for example, textiles, clothing, and food make notably little use of non-strike action.

So far this chapter has been largely descriptive. It now moves on to consider some of the determinants of variations in industrial action, considering first the experience of industrial action and then its frequency.

Determinants of Differences between Establishments

This section looks at the association between a number of factors and the likelihood that an establishment will experience industrial action by manual workers. Non-manual action is considered later. The primary concern is not with which variables explain the greater part of the variance in the number of strikes but with the logically prior question of whether or not strike rates vary across different categorisations of establishment. Besides structural factors, we look at relationships with aspects of both union and management organisation.

Structural Characteristics

In Table 5.5 the proportion of establishments reporting industrial action by manual workers is analysed by five independent variables. As would be expected from previous work (Daniel, 1976:10), there is a pronounced size effect. Two-thirds of plants employing fewer than 100 workers had no experience of industrial action; for plants employing over 1,000 workers the proportion was one-eighth. The tendency for the proportion of plants reporting action to increase with size was almost identical for strikes and other forms of action. The reasons for this will be returned to.

In Daniel's survey, there was a clear link between technology and the occurrence of industrial action. In line with the expectations of Blauner (1964) and others, Daniel found that establishments using mass production and large batch technologies reported action most frequently, with unit and process technologies being least affected by it. The present survey yielded no such neat pattern. It is true that the proportion of plants reporting action was lowest where 'single piece' technologies were used, but all other types of technology were marked by similar proportions reporting action. For strikes alone, plants employing large batch methods reported action most frequently, but process plants were not far behind.

TABLE 5.5

STRIKE EXPERIENCE OF ESTABLISHMENTS BY WORKFORCE SIZE,
TECHNOLOGY, LABOUR COST, UNION DENSITY, AND BARGAINING
STRUCTURE

	Percentage of establishments reporting given action by manual workers		
	Any action	Any strikes	Any other action
Number of full-time employees			
50–99	34	25	15
100–199	44	30	30
200–499	55	38	37
500–999	68	51	53
1000+	86	67	70
Technology			
Process	43	35	29
Mass	45	29	30
Large Batch	49	39	35
Small Batch	50	37	24
Fabrication	44	27	31
Single Pieces	29	10	28
Maintenance	40	27	40
Wages and salaries as percentage of total costs			
0–25	53	37	38
26–45	52	41	21
46–100	38	30	27
Percentage of manual workers who are union members			
0–20	48	45	3
21–40	32	21	13
41–60	36	21	28
61–80	40	29	19
81–100	57	40	42
Most important level of manual pay bargaining			
Multi-employer	48	32	27
Corporate	59	46	37
Establishment	50	38	34
No bargaining	8	4	7
ALL	45.7	32.8	28.7

The possibility that variations in plant size obscured the effect of technology received little support. A classification of plants by technology and size revealed few marked differences in size between process, large batch, and mass production plants. Plants producing single pieces were significantly smaller than average and here a size effect does appear to explain their lack of experience of industrial action. In brief, when size is controlled for, there is no discernible link between technology and experience of industrial action.

The third section of Table 5.5 considers the effect of labour costs on experience of industrial action. Economists since Marshall have argued that workers' bargaining power is particularly great where labour is a low proportion of total cost. Whether this results in a large number of strikes (because workers use their power) or a small number (because concessions are won without the need to strike) remains uncertain. The evidence here supports the former hypothesis since experience of industrial action was greater the lower the proportion of wages and salaries to the total costs. Moreover, when strikes are distinguished from other actions, a large proportion of plants with very low ratios of labour cost had experienced action short of strikes. In other words, pressures such as overtime bans were particularly common where workers were in a strong bargaining position. This finding should be treated with caution in the light of the fact that one third of respondents were unable to estimate percentage labour costs.

There were other possible correlates of bargaining power which we considered. One might expect a skilled workforce to be particularly prone to use sanctions, and one with a high proportion of women to use sanctions rarely. Similarly, the presence of part-time employees might be expected to reduce the amount of industrial action. A number of tests using the proportion of such people in the workforce yielded consistently negative results. Skill, sex, and part-time working do not appear to be related to the experience of strike action.

A further structural factor of possible importance is the level of demand for a firm's products. How does job insecurity influence the propensity to strike? If a firm faces falling demand and has to make redundancies or other reductions in its use of labour, resistance might be expected. On the other hand, knowledge that the firm is in difficulties might reduce militancy either through fear of losing more jobs or because a strike might not be successful. Studies of the trend of strike action have generally supported the latter view; in recessions, the frequency of strike action tends to decline (Pencavel, 1970: 246). The present evidence allows the argument to be tested against cross-sectional as opposed to time-series data. We considered three separate measures of the severity of a fall in demand over the preceding two years: a cut in the labour force, short-time working or other measures to reduce hours, and any fall in market demand. There was a consistent tendency for plants reporting any of the three phenomena to experience more action over the same period than those not reporting them. For example, 28 per cent of factories reporting a reduction in demand had experienced a strike of a day or more, but only 14 per cent of those reporting no fall in demand.

This tendency for an establishment's strike incidence to rise when the demand for its products declines, and when its jobs are in jeopardy, is of considerable significance. The years in question, 1976 and 1977, were ones in which national levels of unemployment remained at the high levels (5.7 per cent and 6.2 per cent respectively) they had only recently attained. One interpretation of the result is that when the economic position of an establishment declines the workforce is reluctant to lower its aspirations and takes action in an effort to maintain the relative pay and effort levels to which it has become accustomed. This supports the finding of Daniel for the period up to 1975 (Daniel, 1976). The fact that our result obtains in a recession suggests that, although a worsening of the general economic climate may reduce the overall frequency of individual action, there is a tendency for such action as there is to be concentrated in those establishments experiencing the recession's most severe consequences.

Union Organisation

An obvious expectation is that a high level of trade union membership will be associated with high levels of industrial conflict. As Table 5.5 shows, such an expectation was only partially borne out. Strikes were actually most common where union density was lowest, and only above the level of 20 per cent unionisation did the proportion of plants experiencing action increase with union density. Establishments in the highest category had significantly more experience of action apart from strikes than did other plants. A high level of density seems to enable unions to organise systematic sanctions such as go-slows and working to rule.

We considered whether this finding reflected an interaction between union density and workforce size. But the operation of any size effect proved to be far from straightforward. Although there was a fairly direct relationship between plant size and union density, there was a more complex one between density and experience of industrial action. Such density effects as were present cannot simply be explained as the indirect results of various size effects.

We explored the possibility of an association between aspects of domestic shop steward organisation and experience of industrial action, and found that there was a fairly clear tendency for experience of action to increase with the extent of steward organisation. Thus experience of action increased with the regularity of shop stewards' meetings. The most notable association was between experience of action *other than* strikes and the presence of a full-time steward. This could not wholly be attributed to an association between plant size and the extent of steward organisation because, as Table 5.5 shows, the proportion of plants reporting strikes and reporting any other actions both rose with increasing plant size. The disproportionately rapid rise in experience of non-strike action with increasing complexity of steward organisation can, therefore, be attributed to a 'real' effect. More complex steward organisation appears to permit greater use of sanctions other than strikes.

Management and Bargaining Structure

The most comprehensive recent theory of strike patterns comes as part of Clegg's international analysis of trade unionism under collective bargaining. It lays special emphasis upon the effect of the bargaining structure: plant bargaining leads to a larger number of strikes than industry or regional bargaining (Clegg, 1976: 82). Clegg also notes the importance of economic circumstances and of relations between unions and the government in determining fluctuations in the number of major strikes, and this makes it necessary to recall the circumstances of incomes policy during the period covered by our question. The two years 1976 and 1977 straddle the three stages of the Social Contract between the Trades Union Congress and the Labour Government. It was, by most standards, a successful period of incomes policy and this influenced the pattern of strikes (Davies, 1979). Whether measured by number of strikes or by number of working days lost, 1976 was the most strike free year of the decade while strike experience in 1977 was about average.

The final section of Table 5.5 gives the incidence of action for different manual pay bargaining arrangements. The proportion of establishments that have experienced either strikes or other industrial action is somewhat smaller where multi-employer bargaining is dominant than where single-employer bargaining prevails. This holds when size effects are allowed for and is consistent with Clegg's theory. More paradoxical is the fact that, among those with single-employer bargaining, both strike and non-strike action is more common where there is a corporate agreement than where bargaining is more fragmented and conducted at establishment level. This is maintained when size is allowed for and when multi-plant establishments are considered alone. A reasonable inference from Clegg's theory would be that corporate agreements, by acting rather like small industry agreements, would be associated with a lower rather than a higher establishment strike incidence than establishment bargaining. Why does this inference not hold?

It is helpful to recall the subjective impressions of establishment industrial relations managers that were discussed in Chapter 3. It was noted that managers in multi-plant firms who reported a relatively low degree of discretion also had above average experience of strike action in their establishments. One possible interpretation was that managers under strike pressures were more aware of the limits to their discretion than those who were not. It was also demonstrated in Chapter 3 that corporate bargaining was associated with perceptions of far less discretion by the managers involved that any other bargaining arrangement. We now complete the triangle with the association between corporate bargaining and strike experience.

Neither perceptions of low discretion nor above average strike experience are likely to 'cause' established corporate bargaining arrangements. Instead it is probable that the subjective feelings of low discretion felt by local managers under corporate agreement do have some objective basis. The metaphor used earlier was that this sort of manager is more a local commissar for the corporate management than a relatively independent negotiator. It will be recalled that the role was associated with below average satisfaction with the attention given to industrial relations matters by fellow managers at his establishment. The relatively high strike experience of establishments covered by corporate agreements thus appears to arise from the restrictions that these and their associated controls place upon local management: they are less able to make *ad hoc* concessions to their workforces than if bargaining was centred on their establishment.

Rates of Industrial Action

We now consider the number of incidents of industrial action; from this it is also possible to estimate rates of activity per 100,000 employees. Figures for the total number of incidents and the number of strikes per 100,000 employees are given in Table 5.6. Similar figures per establishment are given in Table 5.7.

The Size Effect
Perhaps the most notable feature of Table 5.6 is the reversal of the size effect observed in Table 5.5: large plants have fewer strikes *per head* than small plants. Although less well-known than the findings that large plants are more likely to experience industrial action than small ones, this

result accords with previous studies. Paterson (1956: 157) noted a similar phenomenon in his study of the coal industry and a more recent study in the engineering industry (Marsh *et al.*, 1971: 119–20) has provided further confirmation. Indeed, this finding is far from surprising. If several small plants were to employ the same number of workers in total as one large plant, they would have, on simple assumptions about technology and union organisation, a greater number of distinct groups with 'strike potential' than the large plant.

TABLE 5.6

NUMBER OF INCIDENTS OF INDUSTRIAL
ACTION PER HEAD

Number of Full-time Employees	Incidents per 100,000 Manual Employees	
	Total	All Strikes
50–99	1440	958
100–199	1510	466
200–499	842	325
500–999	806	308
1000+	820	372
ALL	992	426

The distinction between the two forms of analysis of Table 5.5 and 5.6 can be made more clear-cut by reference to Table 5.7, which reports the number of incidents of industrial action per establishment. The 'average' plant employing over 1,000 people had over ten times more incidents of action than the average plant employing between 50 and 99 workers. Thus there were more incidents of action in large plants than in small ones and large plants were the more likely to have had *some* experience of industrial action. But they had significantly fewer incidents per worker employed.

These three modes of analysis need to be kept distinct. The numbers of incidents per establishment and per employee, as was noted in the previous section, give quite different impressions of the frequency of industrial action. There are several difficulties with the interpretation of the index of the number of strikes per head, the main one being that the figures do not show the number of times workers used industrial action. The aggregate figure of 992 incidents per 100,000 workers could show that all workers used action together on 992 occasions, or that 992 separate groups used action once each. We shall only use this index again in comparison with non-manual workers.

TABLE 5.7

NUMBER OF INCIDENTS OF MANUAL INDUSTRIAL ACTION PER
ESTABLISHMENT BY WORKFORCE SIZE, TECHNOLOGY, LABOUR COST,
UNION DENSITY AND BARGAINING STRUCTURE

	No. incidents per establishment	% incidents accounted for by:		
		Strikes under 1 day	Strikes 1 day or more	Other Action
Number of full-time employees				
50–99	0.8	51	16	34
100–199	1.8	18	12	69
200–499	2.2	19	19	61
500–999	3.9	23	15	62
1000+	8.8	26	20	55
Technology				
Process	2.3	38	19	42
Mass	2.4	26	18	57
Large Batch	2.2	31	16	54
Small Batch	1.8	17	16	66
Fabrication	1.7	23	16	61
Single Pieces	0.6	8	16	76
Maintenance	2.6	23	5	72
Wages and salaries as percentage of total cost				
0–25	2.9	26	14	60
26–45	1.4	38	21	41
46–100	2.4	23	15	61
Percentage of manual workers who are union members				
0–20	0.5	85	9	6
21–40	0.6	–	36	63
41–60	0.9	23	18	59
61–80	0.9	40	22	38
81–100	2.9	28	17	56
Most important level of manual pay bargaining				
Multi-employer	1.5	43	16	41
Corporate	4.3	13	13	75
Establishment	2.0	25	20	55
No Bargaining	0.3	19	8	72
ALL	2.0	26.5	16.5	57.0

Technology
In line with the results of Table 5.5, there was no clear relationship
between production technology and either index of the frequency of
industrial action that fitted prior expectations. As before, a size effect
is the simple explanation of the lower strike incidence at single-piece
establishments.

Although there is no straightforward relationship apparent between
technology and the frequency of action, there was, as Table 5.7 shows, a
notable tendency for the *form* of action to vary with technology. Single-
piece and fabrication methods were marked by a high proportion of non-
strike actions, with mass and large batch plants having relatively more
strikes, and process plants more still. Given the continuous nature of
production in process plants, and other constraints on striking such as
risk of injury, one might expect strikes to be little used. Not only was
collective action no less frequent than in other plants, however, but
strikes formed a particularly large part of the total.

Part of the explanation lies in the inaccuracy of the common view
that the continuous process plant is typified by the chemicals industry.
Neither is typical of either: only 25 per cent of chemicals plants were
described as continuous process and only 6 per cent of continuous
process plants were in chemicals. Far more continuous process plants
are situated in the food and textiles industries. Whatever the explanation
of the relative frequency of strikes with continuous process technology,
the phenomenon is in clear opposition to the simple view that advanced
technologies inhibit strike activity.

The third section of Table 5.7 suggests an interesting modification of
the Marshallian analysis. There is apparently a U-shaped relationship with
labour cost, with both the frequency of incidents and the preference for
non-strike action being greater when labour cost is either a relatively small
or a relatively large component of total costs. This may suggest that the
greater bargaining leverage enjoyed by workforces in capital intensive
establishments is paralleled by greater strength through solidarity in
labour intensive establishments, with neither advantage accruing to
those workforces in the intermediate technologies. Once again, the high
proportion of 'don't knows' commands caution.

Union Organisation
As Table 5.7 shows, with union density the frequency of industrial
action rises more smoothly than did the experience of it shown in Table
5.5. The form of industrial action also shows a different response to
greater union organisation according to which of these two indicators
one uses. It was noted that higher levels of domestic union organisation

were associated with a greater experience of non-strike action. But when we look at the number of incidents no such effect is evident. The presence of full-time stewards or the holding of regular steward meetings are not associated with a greater preference for non-strike, as opposed to strike, action. The use of *all* forms of industrial action tends to increase with greater domestic union organisation.

The presence of more than one union in an establishment is often seen as a potential source of conflict. Because the number of unions present tends to increase with workforce size, there are difficulties in disentangling a 'multi-union' effect but, by looking at the experience of establishments in different size bands, some conclusions were possible. Multi-unionism does appear to be associated with a high level of industrial action both in terms of the number of incidents per establishment and in the proportion of establishments reporting any action. This finding held true whether or not management reported any problems arising from multi-unionism and whether or not the unions had joint negotiating arrangements. Since, as the previous chapter noted, multi-unionism tends to be associated with greater complexity of steward organisation, the causal connection between it and industrial action is unlikely to be simple.

Management and Bargaining Structure
The variation of frequency of industrial action with different bargaining arrangements is given in Table 5.7. The number of incidents per establishment is over twice as great under corporate bargaining as under the other forms of bargaining. As with the occurrence of action, this holds when size is taken into account. It should be noted, however, that a higher proportion of the incidents experienced by those with corporate agreements take the form of non-strike action. The differences in average strike frequency between bargaining arrangements are slight. There are no substantial relationships between strike frequency and the perceived discretion of managers.

Industrial Action by Non-Manual Workers

The use of industrial action by non-manual workers is largely uncharted and we did not expect it to be very widespread. The survey did indeed show that only 11 per cent of all incidents were carried out by non-manual workers. Only 9 per cent of establishments had experienced non-manual action compared with 46 per cent experiencing action by manuals. But when allowance is made for the numbers employed in the two categories

a rather different picture emerges. Bearing in mind that problems discussed earlier about the measure of the number of incidents per head, we
see in Table 5.8 that there were 363 incidents per 100,000 non-manual
workers; this is slightly over one third the manual figure given in Table
5.5. In manufacturing it thus appears that there is not a massive difference
between the probabilities of manual and non-manual workers being
associated with industrial action. Certainly the finding is far from that

TABLE 5.8

INDUSTRIAL ACTION BY NON-MANUAL WORKERS

	% estabs. reporting any action	Number of incidents per estab.	% incidents accounted for by:		Incidents per 100,000 non-manual workers
			Strikes under 1 day	Strikes over 1 day	
Number of full-time employees					
50– 90	2.9	–	3.4	82.6	287
100–199	3.4	–	–	16.6	255
200–499	15.3	0.4	26.1	23.5	537
500–999	30.2	0.5	14.5	25.1	296
1000+	47.6	1.9	12.0	14.3	332
Number of non-manual workers					
Under 50	4.1	0.1	6.0	40.2	318
50– 99	18.2	0.6	25.6	24.4	890
100–199	18.9	0.3	17.8	18.8	246
200–499	43.2	0.9	11.7	23.9	302
500–999	50.7	1.6	12.5	13.4	247
1000+	69.0	6.4	13.9	12.0	332
Percentage of non-manual workers in unions					
Zero	0.4	–	–	13.9	17
1–25	7.6	0.1	2.7	5.0	191
26–50	15.1	0.3	8.5	13.0	264
51–75	30.1	1.0	25.9	28.5	630
76+	27.1	0.7	14.4	27.3	606
ALL	9.4	0.2	15.9	23.5	363

of the official records on strikes that the number of stoppages per 100,000 non-manual workers was about one-tenth of the rate for manual workers (Smith *et al.*, 1978).

Workforce size and density of unionisation appear, as Table 5.7 shows, to be important influences on non-manual action. The proportion of establishments reporting action increased with size, as did the number of incidents per establishment. Indeed, the size effect was more pronounced for non-manual than for manual actions. This is brought out even more strongly when the number of non-manual workers, and not total employment, is used as the measure of size. Where there were fewer than 50 non-manual workers industrial action was very rare, but where there were over 1,000 the number of incidents per establishment was over three times the average for all manual workers. For non-manuals as for manuals the incidence of action per establishment tends to increase with union density, rather unevenly, and without the strength of the association with increasing workforce size.

Most incidents of action were accounted for by the relatively few plants with large concentrations of non-manual workers. Establishments employing over 200 non-manuals accounted for less than 7 per cent of all establishments but for 43 per cent of all incidents of non-manual industrial action. Where over 500 were employed, the respective figures were 2 per cent and 24 per cent. Being in a large factory and, even more, being in a large concentration of similar workers seems to have had a powerful effect on the non-manual use of industrial action.

In contrast to the findings for manual workers, there was no tendency for the number of incidents of non-manual action per employee to decline as plant size increased. This confirms that it is dangerous to assume that there is a strict link between plant size and the number of groups with 'strike potential'.

The Accuracy of Official Strike Statistics

The footnote to the strike statistics in the Department of Employment Gazette explains that 'they exclude stoppages involving fewer than 10 workers and those which lasted less than one day, except any in which the aggregate number of working days lost exceeded 100. There may be some under-recording of small or short stoppages; this would have much more effect on the total of stoppages than of working days lost.' The problems involved in collecting these data have been analysed in considerable detail (Hyman, 1972; Shalev, 1978; Batstone *et al.*, 1978). But apart from some figures for particular industries, there are no estimates of the size of the under-recording (Turner *et al.*, 1967; Turner, 1969). Our survey therefore attempted a direct investigation by asking respondents about the size of the last strike they had experienced and trying to establish, with the help of the Department's statisticians, whether it had been included in the official statistics.

Those who reported a strike lasting at least a day were asked about its size and duration to establish whether it fell within the official criteria. This procedure may have missed some strikes of less than a day which totalled more than 100 working days lost, but this is unlikely to be a serious omission. In addition, respondents were asked whether the local office of the Department of Employment had been in touch with them about their last strike. The answers to this suggested that such a contact was known about in only 26 per cent of qualifying strikes. But this is misleading. Not only are respondents' memories fallible; more importantly the Department has many means of locating strikes, including press reports and centralised returns from multi-plant organisations.

Consequently it was decided to try to match the strikes mentioned by our respondents with those recorded by the Department. Quite apart from the substantial amount of work required, for which we are greatly indebted to the Department, there were serious technical difficulties. These included the lack of a precise date for strikes reported in the survey, the possible inclusion of strikes officially excluded as being 'political', changes in company name, and the recording of strikes affecting more than one establishment. Thus the matching is unlikely to have been perfect and this is likely to bias the conclusion against the accuracy of official figures.

Particular problems with strike recording in the heavily interconnected vehicles industry led to our omitting it completely. This left 903 establishments of which 332 reported a strike eligible for inclusion in official statistics. Of these, 68 per cent were traced as having been detected and included by the Department's statisticians. In terms of 'working days lost', however, the detection rate is far more impressive. Of the slightly over a million days lost by the stoppages picked up by our survey, the official figures included 97 per cent.

This accuracy of the official figures on working days lost arises from their heavy concentration in relatively few big stoppages. As Table 5.9 shows, while the official figures pick up only 41 per cent of one day strikes, they include 98 per cent of those lasting ten or more days. To put the results another way, of the strikes not recorded, half lasted only one day and three-quarters two days or less. The table also reveals slightly lower detection rate with smaller establishments, largely because they tend to have smaller strikes.

TABLE 5.9

**PERCENTAGE OF ELIGIBLE STOPPAGES RECORDED
BY DEPARTMENT OF EMPLOYMENT BY DURATION
AND ESTABLISHMENT SIZE – UNWEIGHTED DATA**

	Total stoppages recorded in sample	Percentage reported by D.E.
Length of stoppage in days		
1	88	41
2	59	54
3	41	58
4–6	35	91
7–9	26	81
10+	83	98
Number of employees		
50– 99	9	55
100–199	17	47
200–499	91	69
500–999	90	77
1000+	125	65
TOTAL	332	68
TOTAL DAYS LOST	1,006,800	97

The original sample of 970 establishments was a stratified one and the results discussed so far are unweighted. When weighted up to be representative of all manufacturing establishments of 50 or more employees they change slightly. The weighted results are that the official figures record 62 per cent of eligible strikes and 96 per cent of working days lost. These are the first firmly based figures on the extent of under-recording.

The estimate of under-recording can be combined with the actual number of eligible strikes recorded by the Department during 1976 and 1977 to give a figure for the actual number of eligible strikes that must have occurred. The Department's data record 2,836 strikes which implies a total of eligible strikes for the two years of 4,570. Using the evidence presented earlier in the chapter, it is now possible to gross up this figure to produce estimates of the total number of strikes (including those of less than a day) and of the total number of all incidents. When weighted our sample suggested that there were 2.5 times as many strikes of any sort as those of one day or more, and 5.8 times as many incidents of all sorts. If we assume that the official statistics pick up very few strikes which last less than a day but total over 100 'days lost', then the total number of all strikes implied by Departmental data for the two years is 10,700 and the total number of all incidents 26,500. But, even if, as these estimates imply, the actual number of all strikes occurring in manufacturing might be four times greater than the number appearing in official statistics on the restricted definition, the under-estimate of 'working days lost' is still only slight. The smaller the number of days a strike lasts, the smaller the average number of workers involved in it, and three quarters of strikes reported to last between one and two days had fewer than 100 workers involved. If we assume the average strike of less than a day to last half a day and to involve 100 workers, the official figure for 'working days lost' in manufacturing is approximately 94 per cent of the probable actual total.

It is important to distinguish between the validity and the reliability of the data. The validity of a statistical measure is the extent to which it measures what it purports to measure. Thus the official measure of working days lost is highly valid, bearing in mind that it is in no sense a measure of the 'cost' of strikes. The official measure of the number of strikes, however, is not valid in this sense as it substantially under-estimates the number of strikes even on a restricted definition. But this does not mean that it is not a reliable measure. An index is reliable to the extent that repeated measurements under constant conditions will produce identical results. Since recording methods remain much the same, it is probable that the same sort of strikes − notably the larger ones − are regularly picked up. Thus fluctuations in data on the numbers of strikes from year to year are likely to be reasonably reliable indicators of fluctuations in industrial action generally. It is necessary to bear in mind, however, that for manufacturing industry these official figures pick up only approximately two-thirds of eligible strikes and a quarter of all strikes.

Greater caution interpreting official data is, however, necessary when they are broken down to measure strike duration and size effects. Official statistics for all strikes (including those outside manufacturing) for 1976 and 1977 suggest that 18 per cent lasted a day and 14 per cent between one and two days. Our survey results show that, among strikes qualifying for the official definition, the comparable figures are 26 per cent and 18 per cent, and, if we consider *all* strikes, 69 per cent last less than a day. British strikes tend, in international terms, to be even shorter than the official statistics imply.

Similarly, conclusions about the relationship between strike propensity and establishment size need to be modified. The Department of Employment estimated that, during 1971−73, 1 per cent of plants employing between 25 and 99 workers had strikes in any one year; the comparable figure for plants with over 1,000 workers was 44 per cent (Department of Employment, 1976: 1219). Our survey does not permit a direct test, but an indirect indication is possible. Strikes lasting at least a day were reported from 13 per cent of plants with between 50 and 99 workers and from 57 per cent of those with 1,000 or more workers. Thus the effect of plant size on strike-proneness is seriously exaggerated when official data are used.

Conclusion

Although the official statistics on strikes have been shown to provide a good measure of the number of working days lost, their self-confessed weakness in the detection of short and small stoppages has concealed some important features of British industrial relations. One of these is the very widespread use of short strikes and of other collective sanctions across the whole of industry. Another is the considerable use of sanctions by non-manual workers. Our survey has permitted an estimate of the extent of industrial action of all types in manufacturing industry. It has also permitted us to test a number of theories concerning the factors that influence strikes. Popular notions that they are affected by the presence of women and by the production technology have received no support. Instead the analysis has stressed the importance of the size of the establishment and of the bargaining structure by which it is characterised.

6

Personnel and Employment Practice

The ways in which labour is recruited and dismissed, trained and remunerated, are central to the employment relationship and have a powerful effect in moulding workplace institutions. This chapter is concerned with how employers search for new employees, how far they give them additional skills, what payment techniques they use for motivation, and how they dispense with unwanted labour.

Channels of Recruitment

Employers have available a variety of ways of contacting potential recruits. The choice between these is important, not least for the costs which are implied both to the recruiting employer and to the searching worker and thus the speed with which the labour market operates (Stigler, 1962). Previous studies have stressed the importance of informal methods of job search which may, in contrast to some advertising techniques, be almost costless (MacKay *et al.*, 1971; Rees and Shultz, 1970). We investigated this by asking employers which of a series of channels were the main ones they used to find recruits of different skill levels. The definition of skill, to which we shall return, was largely left to the respondent. Table 6.1 gives the responses as percentages of all establishments.

The most commonly used channels are those of the official employment exchange and newspaper advertisements, followed by casual application and recommendations, and by noticeboards either inside or outside the factory. As might be expected, the table shows that the more expensive channels — newspaper, radio and television advertisements and commercial exchanges — are preferred for the more skilled workers. Employers also tend to use a larger number of channels for the more skilled jobs; the average number used for skilled being 3.0 as opposed to 2.4 for unskilled. But it is not only employers' willingness to search harder for more valuable labour that brings about differences between levels of skill. The fact that some skilled workers' unions are able to control the labour market better than those of the less skilled workers shows up clearly in the different use made of their offices as recruiting grounds.

TABLE 6.1

CHANNELS OF RECRUITMENT

Channel of Recruitment	Percentage of Establishments Using the Channel for a Given Skill-Level		
	Skilled	Semi-Skilled	Unskilled
Official employment exchange	77	81	83
Commercial employment exchange	18	10	7
Newspaper advertisements	87	69	52
Notice boards inside or outside	35	36	28
Trade union offices	14	9	7
Applicants just apply, or existing employees recommend people	54	57	57
Radio and television advertising	4	2	1
Any other	10	5	5

The choice of recruitment channel appears to be much influenced by workforce size: Table 6.2 shows this for skilled workers. Noticeboards appear to increase in utility with increased size of establishment. The greater use of informal methods of recruiting in larger factories may reflect the larger 'grapevine' offered by the workforce. The greater use of trade union offices is probably a result of stronger shop steward organisation and the fact, noted in Chapter 4, that full-time union officials tend to maintain closer links with large than with small establishments. That the use of commercial exchanges increases with establishment size and then diminishes over the thousand mark may reflect their tendency to charge on the basis of the number of recruits supplied which means that they do not offer the economies of scale of, for example, newspapers and radio.

There were some interesting industrial differences in preferred recruitment channels. Most idiosyncratic is the printing industry which shuns official employment exchanges and noticeboards to rely heavily upon trade union offices. The distinctive social setting of much of the textile industry if reflected in its being the greatest user of informal methods, noticeboards, and 'other' methods such as door-to-door leafletting. The textiles industry also makes heavy use of commercial exchanges. Second to textiles in use of both informal methods and noticeboards is chemicals. Far and away the greatest user of radio and television is the vehicles industry.

TABLE 6.2

RECRUITMENT CHANNELS AND ESTABLISHMENT SIZE
(skilled workers only)

Channel of Recruitment	Percentage of Establishments by Number of Full-time Employees				
	50–99	100–199	200–499	500–999	1000+
Official employment exchange	73	82	77	79	79
Commercial employment exchange	16	19	20	21	13
Newspaper advertisement	91	83	85	92	86
Noticeboards inside or outside	22	32	49	60	64
Trade union offices	9	14	19	19	26
Applicants just apply, or existing employees recommend people	51	51	56	70	69
Radio and television advertising	1	2	8	7	8
Other	16	4	7	7	5

We explored the choice of expensive recruitment channels by first testing the hypothesis that they not only elicit direct replies but also increase the visibility of the firm in the local labour market and thus stimulate unsolicited applications. The data supported this even when size effects were allowed for. Discriminant analysis was then used to detect characteristics of establishments related to their choice of recruitment channels. More expensive channels were preferred more where there was a higher proportion of women in the workforce and where there was a higher than average proportion of the workforce that management considered difficult to replace. Another significant characteristic of factories using expensive recruitment techniques was that they tended to make less use of apprenticeships and also tended to give the skilled labour they recruited from outside further training within the factory. There was an association between the use of expensive recruitment and comparatively low density of unionisation; it is possible that relatively low pay rates and the absence of trade union recruiting channels contribute to this.

The Acquisition of Skills

For the individual worker one of the most important aspects of a job lies in the extent to which it permits him to acquire and improve skills. Herein lies a crucial source of job interest, job security, and future earning potential. Yet, curiously enough, this has not been a central issue in British collective bargaining, least of all at the level of the workplace. We were interested in how far employers 'buy in' workers with their full range of skills, and how far they train them within the firm or provide them with additional training.

There are a number of definitional problems in asking about this subject across industries with varied practices and terminologies and we opted for the respondent's own definition of 'skilled', prompting, if necessary, with 'one year or more of training before or after recruitment' (the distinction between semi- and unskilled being made at the one month point). Of all full-time manual employees 35 per cent were thus classified as skilled and their distribution by industry and workforce size appears in Tables 6.4 and 6.5. We asked what proportion of the establishment's skilled manual workers had, respectively, come out of the firm's own apprenticeship scheme, been recruited as skilled workers requiring no further training, been recruited as skilled workers requiring some further training and, finally, were recruited not as skilled workers but had since received training. The question obtained a very full response and the aggregate results are given in Table 6.3. The table also indicates the extent to which establishments rely upon the different sources.

The highest proportion, 35 per cent, of skilled workers had been recruited by their present employer with their full complement of skills. Another 21 per cent were recruited as skilled but given further training. Thirty per cent of skilled workers were still employed by the firm to which they had been apprenticed, and the remaining 14 per cent had no apprenticeship but were trained up to their skill by their present employer. Almost two-thirds of all skilled workers in manufacturing industry received either all their training or additional training from their present employer. There can be no doubt that for most skilled workers training is a very important part of the employment relationship.

TABLE 6.3

THE SOURCES OF SKILLED WORKERS

Source of Skill	Percentage of all Skilled Workers from the Source	Percentage of all Establishments for which the Source of Skill Provides:		
		Over 90% of their Skilled Workers	Over 50% of their Skilled Workers	Over 10% of their Skilled Workers
Came from own apprenticeship scheme	30	6	22	50
Recruited as skilled requiring no further training	35	19	39	62
Recruited as skilled but requiring some further training	21	11	22	50
Were recruited not as skilled but have since received training	14	5	16	31
TOTAL	100	42	99	—

This broad spread of employees across the four different sources is, however, misleading as a guide to the practice of individual establishments. The three right-hand columns show that 42 per cent of establishments rely almost exclusively on only one of these sources, and that it is very rare for an establishment not to get at least half its skilled workers from only one source.

The very varied use of the different sources between industries is apparent from Table 6.4. The second row of the table gives the percentage of establishments with their own apprenticeship schemes. Although 61 per cent of all establishments had some sort of scheme, they are concentrated in the engineering and printing trades. A comparison of the first two rows of the table shows a significant positive correlation between the proportion of skilled workers in an industry and its use of apprenticeships. To some extent this is reflected in the proportion of skilled workers still working with the firm of their apprenticeship; it is highest in the mechanical engineering, shipbuilding and metal manufacturing industries. But another force at work is a tradition of mobility of craftsmen between factories in, notably, the vehicles and printing industries. The relatively high proportion of skilled workers still at their place of apprenticeship in the catch-all category 'bricks, timber and miscellaneous' is of interest; it may reflect the strong local traditions of industries such as glass, pottery, and furniture.

Non-apprenticeship training is least common in mechanical engineering, shipbuilding, vehicles, and printing. Metal manufacture, textiles, and clothing are most prominent in training their workers from scratch. Food, chemicals, textiles, and clothing appear to do most to augment the skills of already skilled recruits.

There is a strong association between the size of the workforce and the source of skill. Table 6.5 shows that the proportion of the workforce that management judges to be skilled diminishes with increased workforce size. But large firms are also more likely to 'buy in' fully skilled labour than small firms, and, even allowing for their lesser use of apprenticeships, small firms are more likely to give training to their employees. Fifty per cent of skilled workers in establishments of under 100 employees had received all or further training (excluding apprenticeships) from their own employer compared with 25 per cent of skilled workers in establishments employing 1,000 or more. It suggests that, while there may be economies of scale in running apprenticeship schemes, these do not exist for non-apprenticeship training. For workers over the age of apprenticeship, large establishments would appear to offer relatively poor opportunities for acquiring fresh skills.

TABLE 6.4

SKILLS AND THEIR SOURCES BY INDUSTRY

	Food, Drink, Tobacco	Chemicals etc.	Metal Manufac- turing	Mechanical Engineering and Ships	Instrument and Electrical Engineering	Vehicles	Metal Goods N.E.S.	Textiles	Clothing Footwear etc.	Bricks, Timber and Misc.	Paper Printing and Pub- lishing
% of full-time manual employees defined as 'skilled'	16	26	34	49	25	32	35	37	49	32	44
% of establishments with their own apprenticeship schemes	31	40	78	89	60	85	61	40	57	61	71
Source of Skill – % of all Skilled Employees: firm's own apprenticeship scheme recruited as skilled, no further training	14	23	38	41	26	29	27	17	23	35	30
recruited as skilled but requiring further training	38	33	27	38	36	49	42	19	22	32	43
recruited as skilled but requiring further training	34	35	7	16	19	13	17	31	33	21	19
not recruited as skilled but since received training	15	9	25	5	18	9	15	33	22	12	8
% of full-time manual employees considered difficult to replace	18	21	30	36	28	20	32	43	42	34	36

TABLE 6.5

SKILLS AND THEIR SOURCES BY ESTABLISHMENT SIZE

		Number of Full-time Employees				
		50−99	100−199	200−499	500−999	1000+
% of full-time manual employees defined as 'skilled'		49	42	34	29	30
% of establishments with their own apprenticeship schemes		50	63	71	79	90
Source of Skill − % of all Skilled Employees	firm's own apprentice-ship scheme	22	26	33	28	35
	recruited as skilled, no further training	27	35	34	39	39
	recruited as skilled but requiring further training	28	24	20	22	14
	not recruited as skilled but received training	22	16	13	10	11
% of full-time manual employees considered difficult to replace		38	38	32	30	24

We considered three other possible sources of variation in the source of skills: technology, geographical region and trade union membership density within the factory. Analysis of variance was used, controlling for industry and workforce size. It showed that the practice of training up unskilled recruits was most common for large batch technologies and was least used where the dominant technology was one of single pieces or maintenance. Geographical region was strongly significant in its association with the proportion of skilled workers who were working at the firm of their apprenticeship: Yorkshire and Humberside were highest and the South-East the lowest, a finding that probably owes more to labour mobility than to managerial policy. Finally, a low density of trade unionism in a factory tends to be associated with less 'buying in' of skills and with more training within the firm of workers who had no skills on recruitment. Although this is consistent with the view that trade unions may inhibit the use of non-apprenticeship training, other contributory factors could be the lack of trade union recruitment channels and relatively low pay.

In terms of how the labour market operates, what matters is not simply the extent to which people are skilled, but whether their skills are specific to the enterprise or generally available in the market. Although neo-classical economists such as Becker (1964) and internal labour market theories such as Doeringer and Piore (1971) emphasise the distinction between general and specific skills, the direct evidence is very limited. To find out about this we asked managers 'what proportion of your entire manual workforce possess skills, knowledge or experience which you would find difficult to replace if they left?' There was, as might be expected, a correlation between this measure and the proportion of skilled workers in the establishment, but they were far from identical.

The overall proportion of the manual workforce deemed to be difficult to replace was 29 per cent. Many respondents gave a low figure for the proportion of their employees whose replacement would cause difficulties: 26 per cent stated it to be under 6 per cent, and 38 per cent said under 11 per cent of the manual workforce. As Table 6.4 shows, ease of replacement was highest in the food, chemicals and vehicles industries and lowest in textiles, clothing, and bricks and miscellaneous. Also, as can be seen from Table 6.5, difficulty of replacement was considered to be greater the smaller the workforce, although this is largely a reflection of the relationship with the skill proportion shown in the first row.

Analysis of variance indicated that the variations in recruitment difficulty were not explained by trade union density, geographical region or the size of the local labour market. Instead there was quite a strong association with the form of production technology. Difficulty of replacement and, by implication, enterprise-specific training were greatest with small batch technology and least with mass production.

Payment Techniques

The techniques used in payment are a central feature of workplace industrial relations. They influence the frequency with which there are opportunities for bargaining over both pay and other matters. They also have powerful implications for management controls. Because of the problems involved in classifying different sorts of payment systems and in defining their coverage, we opted for a broad-brush approach, asking about the use of job evaluation, work study, and payment by results, which are probably the three most salient aspects of manual pay systems.

Job Evaluation
Job evaluation is a generic term applied to a variety of methods whereby

the relative pay rates of different jobs within an organisation are established by systematic techniques. These usually involve some analysis of the content of the jobs involved and an assessment of the notions of 'fairness' of relative pay held by members of the workforce. They have been a central feature of the reform of payment systems and the formalisation of workplace bargaining. We asked whether job evaluation was in operation for any significant group of, first, manual, and then non-manual workers, and whether the proportion covered by it had altered over the previous five years.

As Table 6.6 shows, manual job evaluation was present in 43 per cent of establishments and non-manual job evaluation in 32 per cent. Since the technique necessarily covers the whole of a bargaining unit, it appears that 55 per cent of manual and 56 per cent of non-manual workers are in establishments with job evaluation. For both manual and non-manual workers, 34 per cent of the establishments that had job evaluation reported its coverage to have increased over the last five years. Since job evaluation is an 'all or nothing' technique, it is safe to conclude that the number of establishments using it increased by a half between 1972 and 1977. These results on the extent of the technique and its rate of expansion are in close agreement with those derived from the N.B.P.I. (1968) and Daniel (1976) surveys (Brown and Terry, 1978: 128). The implementation of the Equal Pay Act between 1970 and 1975 is likely to have stimulated the spread of the technique.

Table 6.7 shows how both the use of payment techniques and changes in their use vary with the size of the establishment. It is apparent that for both manual, and, very strongly, for non-manual workers, the likelihood of an establishment's using job evaluation increases with its workforce size. Since the technique is a natural feature of the formalisation of workplace industrial relations, this is hardly surprising. Further light on what is happening is cast by the figures showing the net proportion of those establishments with job evaluation that reported its introduction or an increase in their use of it during the previous five years. For manual workers it has tended to be the smaller establishments that have seen most recent development, thus suggesting an evening up in the incidence of job evaluation across establishments of different size. For the non-manuals, on the other hand, it has been the larger establishments that have seen the greatest increase in use of the technique recently. The contrasting incidence of non-manual job evaluation between large and small establishments is thus becoming sharper. Since it has been traditional for non-manual employees to have individual salary rates, this sign of rapidly increasing formality of salary structures is of particular significance. It confirms our earlier findings that in large workplaces, the institutions of collective bargaining that are developing

TABLE 6.6

THE INCIDENCE OF JOB EVALUATION, WORK STUDY AND PAYMENT BY RESULTS BY INDUSTRY

Technique in use in the establishment						Percentage of Establishments						
	All Manufacturing	Food, Drink, Tobacco	Chemicals etc.	Metal Manufacturing	Mechanical Engineering and Ships	Instrument and Electrical Engineering	Vehicles	Metal Goods N.E.S.	Textiles	Clothing, Footwear etc.	Bricks, Timber and Misc.	Paper Printing and Publishing
Manuals												
Job evaluation	43	48	41	38	31	62	55	47	38	51	48	21
Work study	50	40	41	41	56	54	52	46	85	62	37	27
Payment by results	64	41	33	72	76	56	63	70	90	89	56	39
Non-Manuals												
Job evaluation	32	46	37	33	24	55	34	37	16	19	31	30

for non-manual workers are increasingly like those of their manual counterparts.

A number of other characteristics are associated with the use of job evaluation. For both manuals and non-manuals it is considerably more common among foreign-owned than British firms, and among multi-plant as opposed to single-plant firms. The same applies to the establishments where it has seen recent growth. Its use and its increase are linked to large batch technologies. They are also associated with particular forms of bargaining structure, although differently for manual and non-manual employees. For manual workers the use of job evaluation and its recent increase are more common where there is either single-employer manual pay bargaining (whether at establishment or corporate level) rather than where there are multi-employer agreements prevailing. Among non-manuals, however, where multi-employer agreements have never had much sway, job evaluation has moved further, and is moving faster, where non-manual pay is fixed at the corporate as opposed to the establishment level. Job evaluation is also associated with those establishments where the industrial relations function was reported to have grown in importance within management in recent years.

In summary, the use of job evaluation has expanded rapidly among both manual and non-manual workers. This has, for manual workers, been one aspect of the increased formalisation that has accompanied the move to single-employer bargaining. For non-manual workers, on the other hand, it is better seen as an accompaniment to the more recent arrival of collective bargaining on salary matters. This has tended to occur in larger establishments and, aided by the greater inter-plant mobility of non-manual workers, in multi-plant firms, where bargaining has tended to develop at the corporate level. There are also signs that job evaluation owes some of its popularity to the influence of overseas owners, the great majority of whom are American.

Work Study

Work study is concerned with the measurement of labour input. At various times it has also been called time-and-motion study and industrial engineering. Work study can be used for certain aspects of production engineering and financial control, but its most common function is as a basis for payment by results. Only one fifth of the factories we surveyed that reported using work study did not also have some form of payment by results. In practice, the rigour of a factory's work study system can vary greatly and the fact that it exists does not guarantee its effectiveness as a control.

There are, as Table 6.6 shows, work study systems in operation in

50 per cent of manufacturing establishments. Their use was reported to have increased in the previous five years for 32 per cent of establishments. Apart from the heavy use of work study in textiles and its relative rarity in printing, there was not substantial variation between industries. The size of the establishment did, however, prove to be of some importance. As Table 6.7 shows, work study is, as might be expected, more common the larger the workforce. More interesting are the figures on recent increases in its use which suggest that it must be near saturation in the biggest establishments but is still growing in the smallest. Work study was also associated with large batch production, with multi-plant firms, with single-employer bargaining whether at establishment level or corporate level, and with managements who reported a recent rise in status of the industrial relations function. Interestingly enough, it has tended to be British-owned rather than foreign establishments that have seen greater increase in work study in recent years; this probably reflects their different use of payment by results.

TABLE 6.7

USE OF AND CHANGES IN PAYMENT TECHNIQUES BY ESTABLISHMENT SIZE

	Percent of Establishments by Number of Full-time Employees				
	50–99	100–199	200–499	500–999	1000+
Job Evaluation					
Used for manuals	35	45	51	60	51
Net increase in 5 years for manuals	41	27	36	32	23
Used for non-manuals	18	31	44	58	72
Net increase in 5 years for non-manuals	29	27	38	39	49
Work Study					
Used for manuals	38	48	59	74	83
Net increase in 5 years for manuals	44	22	33	31	11
Payment by Results					
Used for manuals	61	68	63	64	62
Net increase in 5 years for manuals	46	13	28	24	12

Payment by Results

Payment by results systems come in many varied forms: some relate to individuals, others to groups or even whole factories; some have a far smaller component of the wage variable than others; some relate pay to output in complex ways. Our definition is, by implication, the broadest possible. The results are correspondingly weak and it would be wrong, for example, necessarily to associate the presence of payment by results as defined here with fragmented workplace bargaining. Although certain forms of payment by results tend to give rise to fragmented bargaining there is evidence that they are on the decline (Lloyd, 1976). An indication of the associated controls is given by the fact that almost two-thirds of the establishments reporting payment by results also reported having work study.

Table 6.6 shows that 64 per cent of establishments have payment by results for some of their manual workers. There is no directly comparable figure from previous surveys from which we can assess whether payment by results is on the increase. Our figure implies that 71 per cent of manual workers are in establishments where at least someone is on payment by results; a comparable figure given by Crossley for 1961 was 73 per cent (Crossley, 1966: 167). This impression that payment by results, despite considerable change between and within industries, has not seen any very substantial increase or decrease overall is in agreement with estimates made a decade earlier (N.B.P.I., 1968: 8). On the other hand, 30 per cent of our establishments (albeit generally the smaller ones) reported an increase in their use of payment by results over the previous five years; it is a proportion that is possibly too large to reflect merely a shift, suggested by Lloyd, to incentive schemes covering larger groups of workers.

The very varied use of payment by results from industry to industry is evident from Table 6.6 with textiles and clothing at one end of the range and chemicals at the other. But the size of the establishment, as Table 6.7 shows, does not seem to be important; the proportion of factories with payment by results is almost constant for all size-bands. Whatever it is that is attractive about this particular motivating device seems equally appealing to management of all sizes of workforce. Nor do other variables discussed so far show any strong associations with payment by results with the exception of the lower use of it by foreign-owned firms and where there are single-piece technologies.

Shedding Labour

Involuntary loss of job can occur through falling product demand, from labour-saving technology, or through dismissal because of some personal failing or misfortune. As an overall average 2 per cent of employees were reported to have been dismissed during the previous two years for reasons not connected with the product market or technology. It would appear that the food industry is particularly hazardous in contrast to mechanical engineering, vehicles, and printing. There is a very strong relationship between plant size and risk of dismissal, with the danger being some fifty times greater in establishments employing fewer than 100 employees than in those with 1,000 or more, a finding consistent with those of Daniel and Stilgoe (1978). We are undertaking a more detailed study of the determinants of dismissal risk; suffice it to say here that the risk diminishes substantially with increases in the proportion of non-manual and skilled workers, and with increasing trade union membership density.

Our principal concern was with the ways in which employers responded to reduced demand for their products or services. The replies indicated that half the establishments had experienced reduced demand at some time during the two years previous to the survey and that just under a half had reduced the size of their skilled, semi-skilled, or unskilled manual workforces. But these two categories were not the same. Under two-thirds of those experiencing a reduction in demand had shed labour, and over a quarter of those shedding labour had had no reduction in demand.

We hoped to establish by discriminant analysis the distinguishing characteristics of those plants which had and had not shed labour from at least two skill categories in response to a fall in demand. No part in the explanation appeared to be played by the percentage of women or of part-time employees in the workforce. Equally surprisingly, no significant part of the variance could be accounted for by the percentage of the workforce in trade unions or by the percentage of the workforce management deemed difficult to replace. Instead, the two significant factors were the technical flexibility of the production process and the size of the workforce. The first of these we ascertained with the question 'if there were a reduction in demand of 10 per cent for your main product, by what proportion could your direct production workers, *technically*, be reduced?' As would be expected, workforce reductions were greater where responses to this question suggested greater technical flexibility. We had no *a priori* expectations as to the effect of workforce size; the analysis showed a significant tendency for workforce reductions to be more likely in larger establishments.

The next concern was with the way in which workforces were reduced. On average employers used between two and three different methods. Generalising for all three skill levels, seven in ten used natural wastage, four in ten used voluntary redundancy, three in ten used enforced redundancy, early retirement, transfers within the organisation, and shedding people over retirement age, and two in ten shed casual and part-time workers. The larger firms were considerably more likely to use voluntary redundancies, early retirement and internal transfers than the smaller. They were also more likely to pay in excess of the minimum entitlement in redundancy payments. One third of firms making people redundant who were entitled to payments had paid in excess although 80 per cent of these payments were no more than half as great again as minimum entitlement.

One reason for firms differing in the extent to which they shed labour in response to a fall in demand was that they might make other adjustments (Thomas and Deaton, 1978). We enquired into the extent to which they built up stock levels and the extent to which they had adjusted the hours worked through overtime reduction or short-time working. Of those firms which reduced their workforce in response to a fall in demand, approximately half also made stock adjustments and three quarters made hours adjustments. Of those reducing their workforce despite no fall in demand, only a quarter built up stocks and less than half made hours adjustments. The only clue that discriminant analysis gave for the causes of these differences in behaviour was that hours reductions tend to be made less where the density of unionisation is greater.

Conclusion

The principal purpose of this chapter has been to provide information about the context within which collective bargaining takes place. In particular it has looked at a number of aspects of current practice on hiring, training, paying and firing workers. In doing so it has drawn attention to the different ways in which employees of different skill levels may be treated, an important question that has been ignored in other chapters. The analysis has added yet more to the already long list of aspects of industrial relations strongly influenced by the size of an establishment's workforce. The discussion of payment techniques has provided further evidence of the rapid recent formalisation in workplace relations and controls.

7

Conclusions

Ten years before our survey, industrial relations in manufacturing industry was dominated by multi-employer agreements. They might have become ramshackle and inadequate, but they were the foundation of the formal bargaining structure. By 1978 that had been transformed. For two-thirds of manual and three-quarters of non-manual employees the formal structure of bargaining has become one of single-employer agreements covering one or more factories within a company. Multi-employer agreements have not vanished. They are still adhered to in many factories with small workforces, and in industries such as clothing and printing which have a large number of small companies, but they cover only a quarter of the manual and a tenth of the non-manual manufacturing workforce.

This change has been so fundamental that it is tempting to see it as the outcome of some concerted strategy. But the truth is more mundane. By the late 1960s the problems that came from informal, fragmented workplace bargaining were painfully obvious to most managements. Whether or not they were aware that they were doing so, they set about following the reforming prescriptions of the Donovan Commission. Our survey shows that there was a great increase in the professionalism of managements' approach. There are now many more specialist industrial relations managers in positions of responsibility than there were a decade ago, and their interests are far better represented on boards of directors. Pay is increasingly fixed by a single bargain for a single bargaining unit, rather than added to on successive bargaining levels. It is also more likely to be covered by job evaluation and by work study. Formal disputes procedures at the place of work have become almost universal. The accumulation of these reforms means that adherence to multi-employer agreements is generally both impractical and unnecessary.

Substantial implications for pay determination arise from the change. Single-employer bargaining, which tends to dominate higher paid industries and to take the lead in the annual pay round, is likely to encourage variation in occupational pay in the labour market. Firms unconstrained by industry-wide agreements are more likely to make settlements that reflect their particular product market circumstances and capacity to pay. The spread of job evaluation will tend to reduce arguments over pay differentials within establishments. But at the same time single-employer bargaining is likely to encourage arguments over comparability between them. The strategic dilemma facing employers — whether to collude in pay determination or to pay what each can afford — is likely to sharpen.

The bulk of single-employer bargaining arrangements take the individual establishment as the bargaining unit. But for a sizeable minority — encompassing a fifth of manual and a quarter of non-manual employees in manufacturing — the arrangements are what we have called 'corporate', covering more than one establishment within the company. In some industries, such as vehicles, corporate bargaining has generally developed out of establishment bargaining; elsewhere, as in food manufacturing, companies appear to have moved straight to it from multi-employer arrangements. Whatever its genesis, and whether or not it is still spreading, corporate bargaining appears to have a distinctive impact upon industrial relations. It raises the level of decision-making on pay (and many other issues) away from the establishment and thus shifts the emphasis of industrial relations management at the shopfloor from negotiation to administration. The frictions that result from this reduced freedom of action would appear to increase the incidence of strikes.

The consequences of the rise of single-employer bargaining for trade unions have been far-reaching. The shop steward has moved from the wings (or prompt-box) to the centre of the negotiating stage. Particularly in larger establishments — and industrial relations practices are acutely sensitive to factory size — stewards now have complex organisations and strong procedural recognition. The emergence of these arrangements has been particularly notable among non-manual workers and in industries where, a decade ago, there was little workplace bargaining.

To some extent the stewards' achievements have come from their own efforts, helped by a more sympathetic attitude on the part of their union leaderships. But the support given to workplace union organisations by management has been enormous. Closed shop arrangements have spread far from their traditional industries and now cover almost a third of the manufacturing workforce; three-quarters of these arrangements are openly supported by management. The deduction of union dues by management, comparatively rare ten years earlier, was in operation for almost three-quarters of union members in manufacturing by 1978. The number of full-time shop stewards probably quadrupled over the decade, so that they now far outnumber the full-time officials on trade unions' own pay-rolls. The proliferation of full-time shop stewardships appears to be particularly dependent upon managerial policy, tending to mirror the degree of specialisation of the industrial relations function. Besides these advances in procedural position and in facilities, workplace union organisations have seen major advances in health and safety committees and in joint consultation.

Despite these apparent improvements to their security, trade unions face fresh causes for concern. Where shop steward organisations have sprung up in factories with little tradition of workplace bargaining, they may owe the superficial sophistication of their facilities and procedures more to the administrative needs of management than to the bargaining achievements of the workforce. It remains to be seen how they will fare in a worsening economic climate. Furthermore, the heavy emphasis that has been placed on formalising the role of shop stewards in recent years makes them poorly equipped to cope with managerial decision-making above the level of the factory. Only half of the establishments covered by corporate agreements were reported as having any sort of combine committee activity.

This study has shown that there have been substantial changes in the contours of industrial relations in manufacturing industry. What lies behind them? One important factor must have been the very rapid increase in trade union membership, rising nationally from 43 per cent of the workforce in 1968 to 54 per cent in 1978. The developments outlined above will have contributed to this growth, just as the growth, especially in non-manual areas, will have encouraged formalisation. Lying behind the growth in unionisation have been increased inflation and increased government intervention in industrial relations (Bain and Elsheikh, 1976). The worldwide inflation that got under way in 1969 was amplified in Britain. The unprecedented price rises that continued throughout the next decade increased pressures both for workers to join unions and for governments to intervene in bargaining.

The managers whom we interviewed were themselves in no doubt that government intervention had had a profound effect, describing it as the principal reason for their increased specialisation in industrial relations matters. Legislative changes seem to have been a major cause, not always intentionally, of the spread of the closed shop, of disputes procedures, of health and safety committees, and the prospect of them may have helped to propagate joint consultation. The surge of concern with incomes policies and labour law has provided a role for employers' associations just as, for many of them, their pay bargaining functions were falling into disuse.

Another underlying change has been the steady increase in the concentration in ownership of British manufacturing industry since the War. The hundred largest manufacturing firms had an average employment of 20,300 in 1958 which had risen to 31,180 in 1972, and undoubtedly continued to rise subsequently (Prais, 1976: 62). British manufacturing firms (as opposed to establishments) tend to be unusually large, larger than their European counterparts (Hannah and Kay, 1977: 120). We have noted that enterprise size appears to influence the specialisation of industrial relations management and, possibly through that, the presence of full-time shop stewards. It is also probable that increased concentration has stimulated corporate bargaining and the withdrawal from multi-employer arrangements.

Foreign investment may also have played a part. Foreign-owned firms (which are predominantly American) appear to be more likely to avoid bargaining altogether than their British counterparts, but when they do bargain they prefer to do it unhampered by multi-employer arrangements. They have a preference for corporate bargaining and for bureaucratic techniques such as job evaluation. The catalytic influence they had in the spread of productivity agreements in the 1960s may have continued with their demonstration of effective single-employer bargaining in the 1970s.

The map of bargaining that we have constructed is one of a constantly changing topography. The driving forces behind the changes in British industrial relations have been those of the changing circumstances of the British economy as a whole: heavy inflation, a worsening foreign trade position, more overseas ownership of industry, growing industrial concentration, and a marked increase in government intervention in employment relations. As the circumstances continue to alter, and, in particular, as the economic decline of manufacturing industry deepens, there is no doubt that these contours will continue to change.

Technical Appendix with Schedule of Questions

The survey was designed to provide a representative picture of manu-facturing establishments with 50 or more employees in Great Britain. There were several reasons for excluding those with fewer than 50 full-time employees. Although such establishments account for over 80 per cent of all manufacturing sites, they employ only 15 per cent of the total manufacturing workforce. They present serious problems for representative sampling and tend to yield poor response rates. Above all, the structured patterns of industrial relations behaviour with which this study is mainly concerned are less common in small workplaces and a high proportion of the questions would be inappropriate.

The fact that employment is concentrated in large establishments presents a problem for structuring the sample. If it were selected randomly from all establishments it would provide relatively little information on the places where the workforce is concentrated or on industries which tend to have large workplaces. The sample had to be designed to permit statements to be made about the characteristics of all establishments, about the characteristics of all employees, and about both of these for specific industries. Accordingly a design was chosen whereby the probability of an establishment's being selected was proportional to its workforce size, and this was then modified to ensure adequate representation of the selected industrial groups.

The budget available permitted a sample size of 970 establishments. Eleven industrial groups were created by merging together some of those in the Standard Industrial Classification which had some degree of technological and institutional similarity. Between 60 and 120 interviews were to be obtained from each of these. Five bands of workforce size were specified from which a minimum of 60 interviews were to be obtained. An added advantage of sampling with the probability of selection being proportional to workforce size is that many aspects of industrial relations of particular interest are more common where there are larger workforces. Consequently more data on matters such as disputes, specialist personnel management and the closed shop are picked up than would come from a simple random sampling of establishments and the effects of over-representation can be corrected by weighting.

Sample Source and Projection

The sample was drawn from the IFF Research Limited File of 45,000 manufacturing establishments. The data come originally from Local Authority Valuation Lists and are regularly updated. The File contains over 70 per cent of manufacturing establishments with 200 or more employees and over 45 per cent of those with between 50 and 199 employees. It is representative within individual SIC industry groups. Establishments were extracted at random from the File according to the required numbers in each cell dictated by the sample design.

TABLE A1

COMPARISON OF SURVEY PROJECTION OF INDUSTRIAL
EMPLOYMENT WITH ACTUAL

SIC Order	Industry	Total 1977 Employment (DE Gazette) (000s)	Estimated 1977 Employment in Establishments of 50 or more (1975 Census) (000s)	Weighted Survey Employment (000s)
3	Food, Drink, Tobacco	705	635	629
4, 5	Chemicals etc.	469	389	381
6	Metal Manufacture	480	432	437
7, 10	Mech. Engineering & Ships	1091	873	901
8, 9	Instrument & Electrical	889	765	755
11	Vehicles	752	745	733
12	Metal Goods N.E.S.	541	379	376
13	Textiles	492	423	428
14, 15 16, 17,	Clothing, Footwear etc.	425	319	332
19	Bricks, Timber & Misc.	859	627	616
18	Paper, Printing & Pub.	537	414	417
3–19	All Manufacturing	7240	6001	6005

TABLE A2

**COMPARISON OF SURVEY PROJECTION OF REGIONAL
EMPLOYMENT WITH ACTUAL**

Region	Manufacturing Employment in Establishments of 50 or more			
	1975 Census		Weighted Survey	
	Number (000s)	%	Number (000s)	%
Northern	414	6.8	207	3.4
Yorks and Humber	614	10.1	621	10.3
South West	353	5.8	265	4.4
North West	897	14.8	1018	17.0
Scotland	542	8.9	448	7.5
Wales	287	4.7	435	7.2
East Anglia	158	2.6	144	2.4
South East	1448	23.9	1698	28.3
West Midlands	872	14.4	824	13.7
East Midlands	484	8.0	346	5.8
Great Britain	6069	100	6005	100

The sample results were projected to a universe of establishments on a matrix of 11 industry by 5 size categories estimated from the official Census of Production. The data used were those of the 1975 Business Monitor (PA 1003) modified to allow for overall changes in manufacturing employment between 1975 and 1977 and for different treatment of part-time employees.

The weighting factors applied consisted of the number of establishments in the estimated size and industry cell universe divided by the number of establishments sampled within the cell. As Table A1 shows the total number of employees projected from the survey establishments was within 0.1 per cent of that of the universe employment estimated, suggesting that there was not apparent sample bias in terms of the average size of establishment sampled within cells. Within the industry groups the difference between prior employment estimate and the sample employment projection was less than 2 per cent for all but one for which it was 3 per cent. Table A2 indicates the generally close regional fit of the sample.

Statistical Confidence Limits

The standard errors of estimates vary considerably according to the type of measurement. Table A3 provides three examples and shows how the standard errors vary with different categories or workforce size. The standard error on a simple attribute of establishments (e.g. the proportion of them reporting manual industrial action) declines with the larger size categories but is comparatively large overall (2.7 per cent in the example). At the other extreme, something that varies in almost direct proportion to the workforce size (e.g. the number of manual shop stewards) gains greatly in precision with the sample design used which picks proportionately more data from size categories with higher variance. A number of intermediate measures lie between these extremes. For example the number of incidents of manual industrial action per establishment increases with establishment size but not in direct proportion to the number of employees.

The figures in the Table provide a rough guide to the magnitude of confidence limits. In general a mean result will stand a 95 per cent probability of being within two standard errors of that which it is estimating. Quite apart from the type of measure under consideration, however, it should be borne in mind that much of the analysis in this study is based upon sub-samples whose size will influence confidence limits.

Response Rate and Biases

The survey was initially piloted by IRRU staff and then by IFF. The sampled establishments were then contacted by telephone for the name of the 'person responsible for industrial relations at the establishment'. In 76 per cent of cases this was a specialist personnel or industrial relations manager and, in the remainder, the member of senior management with responsibility for industrial relations. The questionnaires were filled in during personal interviews lasting on average about one and a quarter hours.

In total 1,457 eligible establishments were contacted and 970 were successfully interviewed, an overall response rate of 68 per cent. Refusals were replaced so as to maintain the sample design. The most common reason for refusal, accounting for 47 per cent of them, was that the respondent was too busy or not available within the time of the survey. A risk of bias was greater from those establishments where no one was able to answer because industrial relations matters were dealt with

TABLE A3

EXAMPLES OF STANDARD ERRORS BY WORKFORCE SIZE

Categories of Workforce Size	Universe		Per cent of Establishments Reporting Manual Industrial Action		Number of Incidents of Manual Industrial Action		Number of Manual Shop Stewards	
	Establishments	Employees (000's)	Mean %	Standard Error on Mean %	Mean %	Standard Error on Mean %	Mean %	Standard Error on Mean %
50– 99	8356	625	34	5.9	0.85	0.29	1.6	0.23
100–199	5558	846	44	4.7	1.79	0.39	2.8	0.22
200–499	4230	1471	55	2.8	2.25	0.26	7.5	0.39
500–999	1326	1011	69	2.7	3.94	0.64	13.3	0.49
1000 +	926	2049	87	1.8	8.82	0.97	43.0	1.94
Total	20397	6005	46	2.7	1.96	0.18	5.8	0.68

from a head office; this accounted for 14 per cent of refusals and was particularly common for small establishments.

The pattern of refusals by industry and workforce size is given in Table A4. The response rate is significantly lower than average in metal manufacturing and textiles. For large establishments in the former and small establishments in the latter our results should be treated with caution. There may be a tendency for our analysis to overstate the extent of industrial relations activity in the smaller establishments because the absence of a manager with responsibility for industrial relations may be related to an absence of employee organisation.

Statistical Techniques Used

Three principle testing techniques were used in the analysis of data. When the variable was simply a category (known as a nominal-level variable), Chi-square tests were used. When it was an actual number (or interval-level variable), analysis of variance was used. Discriminant analysis was used when the object was to explain a nominal-level variable with reference to interval-level variables.

To carry out a Chi-square test the two nominal-level variables whose relationship is in question are cross-tabulated. The test then compares the incidence of data in the table with the incidence that would maintain if there were no relationship between them. It provides a measure of the confidence with which one can reject the conclusion that there is no relationship between the variables.

Analysis of variance provides a means of judging whether an interval-level variable varies significantly across categories of another variable, such as industrial groupings. Or it may provide a means to assess the relative extent to which it varies across two other variables and thus to assess their relative contribution to the explanation of its variation.

Discriminant analysis is used here to distinguish between two groups of a nominal-level variable using a set of observed interval-level characteristics. The objective is to form a linear combination of the discriminating variables in such a fashion that the two groups are as distinct as possible. Variables are entered one at a time; the one that is best at discriminating is used first and the programme stops when the addition of further variables would not help. This provides an indication of which variables are useful for classification and which are not.

These techniques are described in greater detail in the *Statistical Package for the Social Sciences* manual (Nie *et al.*, 1975).

TABLE A4

INTERVIEWS, REFUSALS AND RESPONSE RATE BY INDUSTRY AND WORKFORCE SIZE

		All Manufacturing	Food, Drink, Tobacco	Chemicals etc.	Metal Manufacturing	Mechanical Engineering and Ships	Instrument, and Electrical Engineering	Vehicles	Metal Goods N.E.S.	Textiles	Clothing Leather, Footwear	Bricks, Timber and Misc.	Paper, Printing and Publishing
Total	Interview	970	110	74	76	107	113	67	95	66	78	97	87
	Refusals	487	46	27	61	59	49	28	40	47	40	43	47
	Response %	68%	71%	73%	56%	65%	70%	71%	70%	58%	66%	69%	65%
50–99	Interviews	66	3	6	7	5	4	3	13	1	6	12	6
	Refusals	33	1	1	3	1	2	–	6	4	4	5	6
	Response %	67%	75%	86%	70%	83%	67%	100%	68%	20%	60%	71%	50%
100–499	Interviews	405	41	28	31	37	28	12	42	43	55	41	47
	Refusals	236	28	17	24	17	16	10	12	29	32	19	32
	Response %	63%	59%	62%	56%	69%	64%	55%	78%	60%	63%	68%	60%
500–999	Interviews	242	25	22	24	31	39	12	25	10	10	28	16
	Refusals	121	10	5	13	26	17	7	14	7	4	13	5
	Response %	67%	71%	82%	65%	54%	70%	63%	64%	59%	71%	68%	76%
1000 +	Interviews	257	41	18	14	34	42	40	15	12	7	16	18
	Refusals	97	7	4	21	15	14	11	8	7	–	6	4
	Response %	73%	85%	82%	40%	69%	75%	78%	65%	63%	100%	73%	82%

Schedule of Questions

1. What is the main business activity at this address?

2. How many people in total are employed *full-time* (21 hours a week or more) at this establishment?

3. How many of these are:
   (a) male manual workers?
   (b) female manual workers?

4(a) How many staff would you classify as middle and senior management?
  (b) And how many of these would you describe as *senior* management?

5. How many of the remaining non-manual full-time employees are (a) male? (b) female?

6. How many part-time employees (less than 21 hours a week) work here at the moment?

7. Roughly what proportion of total costs at this establishment are wages and salaries?

8. Which *one* type of production or technology comes closest to the one used most in this establishment?

   Continuous process; mass production; large batch; small batch; fabrication/assemblies; single pieces (not assembly); maintenance/ servicing/repairs; other (specify); Don't know.

9. Is this establishment: a single independent establishment, with no others in the UK?; One of several establishments in the UK belonging to the same organisation or group?

10. Is the organisation: mainly British owned?; mainly owned by an organisation based outside Britain?; Don't know.

SECTION A: EMPLOYERS' ORGANISATIONS

1. Could we turn now to employers organisations. Does your company or organisation affiliate directly to the Confederation of British Industry (CBI), or indirectly, through a national or local employers organisation?

2(a) So far as this establishment is concerned, is your organisation a member of an employers organisation? Yes; No; Don't know.

If Yes

(b) Which employers organisations do you belong to? (WRITE IN)

3(a) Do they (any of them) have an external disputes procedure relating to industrial relations problems which you are able to make use of? Yes: No: Don't know.

If Yes to 3a

3(b) How many times have you referred issues to this procedure in the last 2 years?

3(c) Would you say you use this procedure more, less or about the same as you did 5 years ago?

4(a) Which of these advisory or information services, if any, do the employers' organisation you belong to provide?

If any provided

(b) and which has this establishment actually made use of in the past 2 years?
    recruitment advice/information
    education/training advice/information
    labour legislation, law
    work study/bonus schemes
    job evaluation
    redundancy policy
    local pay levels
    incomes policy

If any used

(c) In general would you say your use of these services in the past few years has: decreased, stayed the same, or increased.

5. *If NOT a member of employers organisation*
Has your organisation ever been a member of an employers organisation relevant to your industry?

If Yes, how long ago? _____

SECTION B: TRADE UNIONS

I now want to ask you a number of questions about trade unions in this establishment.

1. Firstly, are any manual workers employed here members of trade unions? Yes: No: Don't know.

   If Yes

2(a) Approximately what proportion of the full-time manual employees are members of unions?

  (b) Are any manual unions in this establishment recognised by management for negotiating pay and conditions?

   If Yes

  (c) Which unions are they? If more than 3 ask for 3 largest.

   If more than one

3(a) Do they negotiate over major issues jointly or separately? Jointly; independently/separately.

  (b) Have any problems occurred between the different manual unions over the past 2 years?

   If Yes to 3(b)

  (c) What kind of problems?

   ASK ALL WITH RECOGNISED MANUAL UNIONS

4(a) In practice do any manual workers here have to be union members in order to keep their jobs?

   If Yes

  (b) Roughly what proportion of manual jobs fall into this category?
  (c) Is this practice supported by an arrangement or agreement with management? Yes: openly; Yes: tacitly; No; Don't know/refused.

  (d) How long has this been in effect?

  (e) What advantages, if any, do you think this has for management?
  (f) And what disadvantages, if any?

   ASK ALL WITH RECOGNISED MANUAL UNIONS

5(a) Do you have any system for deducting manual employees union dues direct from their pay? (Deduction at source/check off).

   If Yes

  (b) How many years ago was this started?

6(a) Do the manual unions have shop stewards or union representatives here (apart from Health & Safety Representatives)?

If Yes

(b) Roughly how many?

(c) Do they ever represent workers belonging to other unions apart from their own?

(d) Are any recognised or acknowledged by management as senior representatives or convenors?

7(a) Are there any who consistently spend more or less all of their time, in practice, on work-place union affairs? THIS ONLY COVERS EMPLOYEES PAID BY THE COMPANY AND NOT FULL-TIME UNION OFFICIALS PAID BY THE UNION.

If Yes to 7(a)

(b) Roughly how long has this been the case?

(c) How many such representatives do you have now?

ASK ALL WITH MANUAL STEWARDS OR REPS.

8(a) Do manual shop stewards or representatives hold meetings amongst themselves with no other participants? Yes: regularly; Yes: occasionally; No: never; Don't know.

If Yes

(b) Do these meetings ever involve stewards from more than one union? Yes: regularly; Yes: occasionally; No: never; Only one union here; Don't know.

IF ESTABLISHMENT IS NOT SINGLE, INDEPENDENT ESTABLISHMENT

9. Do meetings take place between manual union stewards or representatives from here and shop stewards working in other parts of your organisation? THESE MAY BE CALLED COMBINE COMMITTEES. Yes: regularly; Yes: occasionally; No: never; Don't know.

ASK ALL WITH MANUAL STEWARDS OR REPRESENTATIVES

10. How often does management above foreman level meet manual stewards or representatives to discuss work-place industrial relations?

Once a month or more often on a regular basis.
Once a month or more often but not on a regular basis.
Less than once a month, on average.
Never.
Don't know.

11. From the point of view of management, how important are external full-time trade union officers from manual unions to industrial relations here? (THESE ARE OFFICIALS PAID BY THE UNION)
Very important: they always take the lead
Fairly important: they sometimes take the lead
Not very important: they rarely play an important part
Not at all important
Don't know

ASK ALL

12(a) Are any non-manual workers here members of trade unions?

(Repeat of Manual Questions for Non-Manual: 12(b) as 2(a); 13 as 2(b), (c); 14 as 3; 15 as 4; 16 as 5; 17 as 6; 18 as 7; 19 as 8(a); 20 as 9; 21 as 10; 22 as 11)

ASK ALL WITH UNIONS

23(a) In general are there any ways in which management has put its relationship with shop stewards or representatives on a more informal basis in the last 5 years?

If Yes

(b) Could you describe what changes have been made. (PROBE INCLUDING ANY DIFFERENCES BETWEEN MANUAL AND NON-MANUAL)

ASK ALL

24. Are there any *non-union* employee representatives here apart from exclusively Health & Safety representatives? Yes: manual workers; Yes: non-manual; No; Don't know.

25(a) Do you have a joint management and employee *committee* set up just to deal with Health & Safety matters?

(b) Was this introduced after the publication of the Health & Safety at Work Bill in 1974?

ASK ALL

26(a) Do you have any other joint committees of managers and employees here which are primarily concerned with *consultation* rather than negotiation?

   If Yes

(b) Have these been introduced within the last 5 years?

(c) Are the employee representatives chosen through trade union channels? Yes: all; Yes: some; No; Don't know.

(d) From a management point of view, would you say the operation of the Committee/Committees is: very successful; usually successful. occasionally successful; not very successful; don't know.

SECTION C: PAY AND CONDITIONS SETTLEMENTS

1(a) Here is a list of industry-wide agreements between employers and trade unions. Do you follow any of these for manual workers at this establishment? (SHOW LIST)

   Interviewer's note: Any agreement which affects the pay of your workers directly or indirectly because you normally follow all or some parts of the changes in terms and conditions brought about by it.

   If Yes

(b) Which one? (IF SEVERAL, INDICATE THE ONE WHICH APPLIES TO MOST WORKERS)

   ASK ALL

(c) Are there any others not listed? Which ones? INDICATE ONE APPLIED TO MOST WORKERS.

   IF ANY AGREEMENT MENTIONED IN Q1

2. In *normal* years, which of these is closest to the way that the industry-wide agreement on basic wage-rates is applied? (NORMAL means in the absence of Incomes Policy)

   IF SEVERAL AGREEMENTS OPERATE ASK FOR ONE COVERING MOST WORKERS

   basic wage-rates of industry-wide agreement normally adhered to directly

   industry agreement basic is lower than rate paid here but pro-rata increases above this are normally given

basic rates of agreement are normally only applied to prevent earnings falling below a specified minimum

industry agreement basic rates not applied at all, although agreement may influence other elements of pay (e.g. covering overtime rates, shift premiums)

agreement does not normally affect pay at all although it may affect other conditions of work (e.g. normal working week)

Other (specify)

Don't know

ASK ALL

3(a) Could we now talk about the last pay settlement you made with any major group of manual workers? EXCLUDE ANY SETTLE-MENTS NOT YET FINALISED BUT INCLUDE ANY FINALISED BUT NOT IMPLEMENTED.

Were all manual workers involved or only some of them?

If only some

(b) Which manual workers were they?
(c) How many were involved?
(d) Under which stage of incomes policy was it made?
    £6 limit; 5% or £2.50 − £4 limit;
    Current guidelines 10%; Don't know.

ASK ALL

4(a) At which of the following levels were negotiations or discussions conducted which affected this settlement?

If any negotiations or discussions

(b) Were there any other negotiations or discussions?

If more than one mentioned in 4(a) or (b)

(c) And which would you say was the most important? (E.G. GAVE RISE TO LARGEST PART OF INCREASE)

Negotiations through a statutory wages board or council

Industry-wide agreements involving more than one employer

Regional or district negotiations involving several local employers

Negotiations at your group or total organisation level also covering similar workers elsewhere in the organisation or group

Negotiations at divisional level of your organisation or group

Negotiations or discussions covering only workers employed here at this establishment

Other negotiations or discussions (specify)

No negotiations or discussions between employers and workers or their representatives

Don't know

ASK ALL

5. Have you any intention of introducing a productivity scheme during the present period of Incomes Policy guidelines? No; Yes — have already decided/introduced; Yes — possibly; Don't know. Comments:

ASK ALL

8(a) Could you tell me which, if any, of these forms of industrial action have actually taken place here in the last 2 years, firstly by *manual* workers? and secondly, by non-manual workers?

For each mentioned as for manual and non-manual separately

(b) How many times has a . . . (type of action) occurred here involving . . . manual/non-manual workers in the last 2 years?
   Strike of *less* than a day/less than a whole shift
   Strike of one day/one shift or more
   Overtime ban/overtime restriction
   Work to rule
   Go slow
   Work in/sit in
   Other types of industrial action (please specify)

IF STRIKE OF A DAY/SHIFT OR MORE HAPPENED AT ALL IN LAST 2 YEARS — (Others Go to Q10)

9(a) On the last occasion you had a strike of a day/shift or more, roughly how many workers took part directly?
   (b) And how many days did it last?
   (c) Were any other employees *here* laid off as a result?
   (d) Roughly how many?
   (e) How long for?

IF COMPLICATED, ASK ROUGHLY HOW MANY WORKER DAYS LOST THROUGH LAY-OFF

ASK ALL WITH STRIKE OF A DAY OR MORE

(f) Was the local Department of Employment office in contact with you over this strike?

ASK ALL

10(a) Do you have procedures for dealing with disputes over pay and conditions of work?

If Yes

(b) Do these procedures have provisions for intervention from ACAS or some other body from *outside* the industry? (NOT EMPLOYERS ASSOCIATIONS OR UNIONS, ETC.)

If Yes

11(a) Are the provisions for outside intervention substantially the same for all workers here or do they differ for different groups? (E.G. MANUAL & NON-MANUAL DIFFERENT)

Substantially the same for all; differ for different groups (specify).

IF DIFFERENT ASK THE FOLLOWING QUESTIONS FOR THE LARGEST GROUP OF WORKERS COVERED WHERE PROCEDURE FOR OUTSIDE INTERVENTION EXISTS, SPECIFYING WHICH GROUP THIS IS

(b) Is this procedure written or oral? TRY AND OBTAIN COPY IF WRITTEN

(c) Was it negotiated *and* agreed with trade unions/staff associations? Yes: formally agreed; Yes: accepted but not formally agreed; No; Don't know.

12(a) Who provides the service? ACAS other (specify).

(b) Which of these functions does . . . provide under your procedure? IF IN DOUBT OVER CONCILIATION OR MEDIATION, CODE CONCILIATION. Conciliation; Mediation; Arbitration.

If arbitration mentioned – (Others go to Q13)

12(c) Is the arbitration by agreement between the parties or can it be initiated by one party alone? Agreement; one party alone; depends; Don't know.

13(a) In practice has third party intervention from ... usually been avoided despite the terms of the procedure?

> Avoided in practice
> Not avoided in practice
> Disputes never gone that far
> Don't know.

(b) In the past 2 years have you in fact used ... for a dispute over pay and conditions under this procedure?

If Yes

(c) In the last case, did they bring about a resolution of the dispute? Yes; No; Not yet resolved; Don't know.

(d) How satisfied were you with their intervention?

> Very satisfied; fairly satisfied; not very satisfied; not at all satisfied; Don't know.

NOW GO TO SECTION D

ASK ALL THOSE WITH NO PROCEDURE WHICH LEADS TO OUTSIDE INTERVENTION

(No or Don't know to Q10(a) or 10(b))

14. In the last 2 years have you had a dispute over pay and conditions here which resulted in outside intervention from ACAS or some other body outside the industry?

If Yes

15(a) Who provided the outside intervention? ACAS; Other (specify); Don't know.

(b) Which function did they provide? IF IN DOUBT OVER CONCILIATION OR MEDIATION, CODE CONCILIATION. Conciliation; Mediation; Arbitration.

(c) Did they bring about a resolution of the dispute? Yes; No; Not yet resolved; Don't know.

(d) How satisfied were you with their intervention? READ OUT Very satisfied; fairly satisfied; not very satisfied; not at all satisfied; Don't know. Comments:

———————————

SECTION D: TRIBUNALS AND CONCILIATION, ETC.

May we now talk about cases of alleged unfair dismissal you have been
involved in:

1(a) In the last 2 years, how many people have been dismissed apart
from any made redundant?

(b) And how many, if any, have been made redundant? (DO NOT
INCLUDE VOLUNTARY REDUNDANCY)

IF ANY IN 1(a) or 1(b) — Others go to Q6(a)

2(a) Has any employee or ex-employee, in the last 2 years, *started* a
tribunal action against the organisation on the grounds of unfair
dismissal (including constructive dismissal and unfair selection for
redundancy)?

If Yes

(b) How many cases have been *started*?

(c) Were any of these on the grounds of unfair selection for redundancy?

If Yes

(d) How many?

3. How many (of all the cases):

(a) Went to a hearing?
(b) Were settled or withdrawn without a hearing?
(c) Have not yet been concluded?

IF any in 3(a) or 3(b) — (if none in (a) or (b) go to Q6)

4(a) Could you tell me about the last case you know about to reach a
conclusion, whether it went to a hearing or not?
Did the case actually go to a tribunal hearing?

If Yes

(b) What was the outcome of the tribunal?

Case dismissed/found for the company
Reinstatement of employee in same job
Re-engagement of employee in a different job
Monetary compensation awarded
Found for employee but parties left to agree settlement

Other (specify)
Don't know

(c) Did the case go to appeal?

If Yes

(d) What was the outcome of the appeal?

If No to Q4(a)

5(a) (In the last case which did not go to a tribunal hearing) what was the outcome?

Applicant dropped the case without a settlement
Applicant was reinstated in old job
Applicant was re-engaged in a different job
Applicant was given a monetary payment
Other (write in)
Don't know

(b) Was a conciliation officer from ACAS (Advisory, Conciliation and Arbitration Service) involved?

If Yes

(c) Do you think you would have been able to reach agreement without the involvement of an ACAS conciliation officer?

ASK ALL

6(a) Do you have established procedures to deal with disputes over discipline/dismissal other than redundancy?

If Yes

6(b) Is the procedure the same for all workers here?

If No

(c) Could you tell me about the procedure covering the largest group of workers?

ASK ALL WITH PROCEDURES FOR DISCIPLINE/DISMISSAL

7. Which of these statements applies to this procedure?

(a) procedure is written
(b) procedure was negotiated and agreed by management and unions/employees
(c) procedure has provision for intervention from ACAS in the event of failure to agree

(d) procedure has provision for intervention from some other body (not Employers Association or unions) in the event of failure to agree.

IF NEITHER (c) nor (d) go to 10(a)

If Yes: From whom?

If Yes to 7(c) or 7(d) – (Others go to Q10(a))

8(a) Which of these services does the outside body provide under this procedure? IF RESPONDENT NOT SURE IF CONCILIATION OR MEDIATION, ASSUME CONCILIATION. Conciliation; Mediation; Arbitration.

If Yes to arbitration – (Others go to Q9(a)

(b) Do both sides have to agree to arbitration or can either side apply without the other agreeing?

9(a) Have you had a dispute over discipline/dismissal in the last 2 years which actually used this outside intervention?

(b) In practice has outside intervention usually tended to be avoided despite the terms of the procedure?

NOW GO TO QUESTION 11(a)

IF NO THIRD PARTY PROVISION OR NO PROCEDURE AT ALL

10(a) In the last 2 years, have you in fact used intervention from outside the industry to try and settle a dispute over discipline/dismissal (other than as a result of an application to a tribunal)?

If Yes

(b) Who provided this service on the last occasion?

(c) Which function did they provide? Conciliation; Mediation; Arbitration; Don't know.

ASK ALL WITH DISCIPLINE/DISMISSAL PROCEDURE

11(a) Do you have established procedures for dealing with individual grievances?

If Yes

(b) Does this procedure differ from the discipline procedure (for this group) in any of the points that we covered?

ASK ALL WITH NO DISCIPLINE PROCEDURES

(Repeat of Discipline/Dismissal Questions for Individual Grievances: 12 as 6; 13 as 7; 14 as 8; 15 as 9; 16 as 10)

17(a) Does your organisation as a whole have any policy regarding the use of ACAS?

   If Yes

   (b) What is the policy? PROBE FOR POLICY AND IF ANY DIS-CRETION POSSIBLE FOR INDIVIDUAL MANAGERS/ESTABLISHMENTS

   ASK ALL

18(a) Do you, yourself, think that ACAS is an independent service?

   If Not

   (b) Why not?

   ASK ALL

19.   Do you, yourself, think there is a need for an independent conciliation and arbitration service?

―――――――――

SECTION E: EMPLOYMENT POLICY AND PRACTICE

   ASK ALL

 1(a) Could you tell me which of these are in operation here as far as any significant group of manual workers is concerned?

   For each in use

   (b) Over the past 5 years would you say the proportion of manual workers covered by ... (job evaluation/work study/PBR) has increased, stayed the same, or decreased?

   job evaluation; work study; payment by results

   ASK ALL

 2(a) Is any job evaluation in operation here for any significant group of non-manual workers?

   If Yes

   (b) Over the past 5 years has the proportion of non-manual workers subject to job evaluation increased, stayed the same or decreased?

   ASK ALL

3. Could you tell me what proportion, or how many, of your manual workers are: skilled workers; semi-skilled; unskilled

   NOTE: RESPONDENTS PERCEPTIONS OF CATEGORIES ARE REQUIRED BUT IF UNABLE TO CATEGORISE SAY SKILLED = 1 YEAR OR MORE OF TRAINING BEFORE OR AFTER RECRUITMENT; SEMI-SKILLED = 1 MONTH BUT LESS THAN A YEAR'S TRAINING; UNSKILLED = UNDER 1 MONTH'S TRAINING. INCLUDE IN EACH THOSE UNDER-GOING TRAINING FOR THEIR RESPECTIVE CATEGORY. IF IN DOUBT, CLASSIFY AS SEMI-SKILLED.

4. What are the main methods you use to find recruits for . . . (each category of skill given below)?

   > official employment exchanges
   > commercial employment exchanges
   > notice boards inside or outside
   > newspaper advertisements
   > trade union offices
   > applicants just apply/existing employees recommend people
   > radio or television advertising
   > any other (specify)

   For each type of worker

5. Roughly how long would you expect it to take for a typical new adult recruit to reach full productivity for a . . . skilled/semi-skilled/unskilled? WRITE IN IN DAYS/WEEKS/MONTHS

6(a) Does your establishment have a *formal* training programme with off-the-job elements for any new recruits? THIS INCLUDES ANY INDUCTION TRAINING BUT INDICATE IF THIS IS ONLY INDUCTION TRAINING.

   If Yes

   (b) Does this cover . . . (type) recruits?

   For each type mentioned in 6(b)

6(c) On average how many days training does this programme consist of for a . . . recruit?

   IF ANY SKILLED MANUAL WORKERS AT ESTABLISHMENT
   – Others go to Q8

7. What proportion of your skilled manual workers have:

   (a) come out of your own apprentice scheme
   (b) were recruited as skilled workers requiring no significant further training
   (c) were recruited as skilled workers requiring some further training
   (d) were recruited *not as skilled workers* but have since received training
   (e) other (specify)

   ASK ALL

8. What proportion of your *entire manual* work-force possess skills, knowledge or experience which you would find difficult to replace if they left?

9(a) Has your establishment, in the past 2 years, recruited adult manual workers who were not immediately required but who would be needed later?

   If Yes

   (b) Why was this? Training purposes; Other (specify)

   ASK ALL

10(a) Do you ever use sub-contract manual labour here, apart from for maintenance and construction work?

   If Yes

   (b) Is this:
      a regular feature of your operation
      to increase your manpower for a short-term need
      other (specify
      don't know

   ASK ALL

11(a) If there was a reduction in demand of 5% for your main product here, by what proportion could your direct production workers, *technically*, be reduced?

   This question is only concerned with the way your *technology* operates and how far jobs are inter-connected. Please do not consider other factors apart from the technical which might, in practice, prevent you from reducing direct production workers.

(b) What effect on direct production workers would a 10% reduction in demand have?

(c) And a 20% reduction in demand?

For each where any % of direct production workers reduced: would this reduction involve the cutting out of a whole production line or shift?

ASK ALL

12. Apart from normal seasonal variations, has this establishment experienced a reduced demand for its products or services at any time in the past 2 years?

13. Have you at any time in the past 2 years reduced the size of your: (a) skilled manual workforce; (b) semi-skilled; (c) unskilled manual workforce?

For each category where Yes to Q13 – (If none go to Q16)

14. Which of these methods did you use for . . . (type of workers)?

> shedding casual or part-time labour
> early retirement
> voluntary redundancy
> enforced redundancy
> transfer of people to other parts of the organisation
> stopped recruiting/not replacing leaving workers
> shedding workers over retirement age
> other (specify)

If voluntary or enforced redundancy mentioned for any category – (Others go to Q16(a))

15(a) In the past 2 years how many manual workers volunteered/have been made redundant?

(b) How many were *not* entitled to statutory redundancy payments?

If any not entitled

(c) How much, if anything, did they receive?

If any entitled to statutory pay – (Others go to Q16(a))

(d) What was the total cost of redundancy payments made to those legally entitled to redundancy pay?

(e) And what proportion of this, if any, was over the minimum required by law?

ASK ALL

16(a) Could you tell me which of these measures, if any, you have taken in the last 2 years?

(b) Which, if any were taken: (i) to avoid reducing your workforce, or, (ii) as a result of industrial action or interruptions in supplies?

> short-time working
> reduction in overtime
> built up stocks of finished goods
> reduced work-rates
> temporarily laid off workers

SECTION F: INDUSTRIAL RELATIONS MANAGEMENT

ASK Q1 FOR THOSE THAT ARE NOT SINGLE, INDEPENDENT ESTABLISHMENTS – (Others go to Q2)

1(a) Is this the UK headquarters of the *entire* organisation you belong to?

If NO

(b) Is there a specialist personnel and industrial relations function at some higher level in the group or organisation?

(c) How much discretion would you say that management at this establishment has over settling matters concerned with:

> (a) training policy
> (b) manual workers' pay
> (c) junior management pay
> (d) redundancies
> (e) dismissals
> (f) industrial relations matters generally.

>> (i) complete or almost complete freedom
>> (ii) considerable discretion within broadly defined rules or advice
>> (iii) limited discretion within fairly detailed rules
>> (iv) virtually no freedom.

(d) In the last 5 years would you say the amount of discretion allowed to management here by the wider organisation has increased, stayed the same, or decreased on matters of (a) pay, and (b) other terms and conditions of employment?

ASK ALL

2(a) Is there a director or someone at the highest level of the organisation whose specific responsibility is personnel and/or industrial relations?

If Yes

(b) Is this his/her *sole* responsibility?

ASK ALL

3. Is personnel and/or industrial relations your main area of responsibility; E.G. RESPONDENT NOT RESPONSIBLE FOR PRODUCTION, MARKETING, SALES, FINANCE, ETC., NOR GENERAL MANAGEMENT.

If Yes to Q3

4. How satisfied are you that the management at this establishment generally:

   (a) takes heed of industrial relations policies, procedures and agreements.
   (b) seeks appropriate advice from you/your department on industrial relations matters.
   (c) passes on relevant information to you/your department about events here.

   (i) very satisfied
   (ii) fairly satisfied
   (iii) not very satisfied
   (iv) not at all satisfied
   (v) don't know
   (vi) N/A

ASK ALL

5. How influential would you say that personnel and industrial relations considerations are in formulating policy and making decisions in this organisation on the following;

   (a) fixed capital investment decisions
   (b) major changes in production methods
   (c) wages and conditions of employment
   (d) decisions to make employees redundant

    (i) play the central role
   (ii) heavily involved
  (iii) consulted
  (iv) not involved at all
   (v) don't know
  (vi) N/A

ASK ALL

6(a) Would you say that the position of the industrial relations function here, in the last 5 years, has become much more important, more important, stayed about the same, become less important?

If much more or more important

(b) Why do you think this is?

ASK ALL

7(a) What has been the most important change in the conduct of industrial relations here in the last five years?

(b) Have you any other comments to make about industrial relations?

References

Advisory, Conciliation and Arbitration Service (1980), *Annual Report 1979*, London: HMSO.

Bain, G.S., and F. Elsheikh (1976), *Union Growth and the Business Cycle: An Econometric Analysis*, Oxford: Basil Blackwell.

Bain, G.S., and F. Elsheikh (1980), 'Unionisation in Britain: An Inter-Establishment Analysis Based on Survey Data', *British Journal of Industrial Relations*, XVIII, 169–78.

Batstone, E.V., I. Boraston and S. Frenkel (1977), *Shop Stewards in Action: The Organization of Workplace Conflict and Accommodation*, Oxford: Basil Blackwell.

Batstone, E.V., I. Boraston and S. Frenkel (1978), *The Social Organization of Strikes*, Oxford: Basil Blackwell.

Becker, G.S. (1964), *Human Capital*, New York: Columbia.

Blauner, R. (1964), *Alienation and Freedom*, Chicago: University of Chicago Press.

Boraston, I., H. Clegg and M. Rimmer (1975), *Workplace and Union*, London: Heinemann.

British Institute of Management (1972), *The Board of Directors*, London: BIM.

Brown, W.A., and K. Sisson (1975), 'The Use of Comparisons in Workplace Wage Determination', *British Journal of Industrial Relations*, XIII, 23–53.

Brown, W.A., R. Ebsworth and M. Terry (1978), 'Factors Shaping Shop Steward Organisation in Britain', *British Journal of Industrial Relations*, XVI, 139–59.

Brown, W.A., and M. Terry (1978), 'The Changing Nature of National Wage Agreements', *Scottish Journal of Political Economy*, XXV, 119–34.

Clegg, H.A. (1976), *Trade Unionism Under Collective Bargaining*, Oxford: Basil Blackwell.

Clegg, H.A., A.J. Killick and R. Adams (1961), *Trade Union Officers*, Oxford: Basil Blackwell.

Commission on Industrial Relations (1972), *Employers' Organisations and Industrial Relations*, Study No. 1, London: HMSO.

Commission on Industrial Relations (1973), *Industrial Relations at Establishment Level: A Statistical Survey*, Study No. 2, London: HMSO.

Crossley, R. (1966), 'Collective Bargaining, Wage-Structure and the Labour Market in the United Kingdom', *Wage Structure in Theory and Practice: Three Studies*, ed. E.M. Hugh-Jones, Amsterdam: North-Holland Publishing Co.

Daniel, W.W. (1976), *Wage Determination in Industry*, London: PEP.

Daniel, W.W. and E. Stilgoe (1978), *The Impact of Employment Protection Laws*, London: PSI.

Davies, R.J. (1979), 'Economic Activity, Incomes Policy and Strikes: A Quantitative Analysis', *British Journal of Industrial Relations*, XVII, 205–23.

Deaton, D.R., and P.B. Beaumont (1980), 'The Determinants of Bargaining Structure: Some Large Scale Survey Evidence for Britain', *British Journal of Industrial Relations*, XVIII, 202–16.

Department of Employment (1971), *The Reform of Collective Bargaining at Plant and Company Level*, Manpower Paper 5, London: HMSO.

Department of Employment (1976), 'Distribution and Concentration of Industrial Stoppages in Great Britain', *Department of Employment Gazette*, LXXXIV, 1219–24.

Department of Employment (1977), 'Stoppages of Work Due to Industrial Disputes in 1976', *Department of Employment Gazette*, LXXXV, 579–86.

Department of Employment and Productivity (1970), *New Earnings Survey 1968*, London: HMSO.

Doeringer, P.B., and M.J. Piore (1971), *Internal Labor Markets and Manpower Analysis*, Lexington, Mass.: Heath.

Edwards, P.K. (1980), 'Size of Plant and Strike-Proneness', *Oxford Bulletin of Economics and Statistics*, XLII, 145–56.

Edwards P.K. (1981), 'The Strike-Proneness of British Manufacturing Establishments', *British Journal of Industrial Relations*, XIX (forthcoming).

Flanders, A. (1970), *Management and Unions*, London: Faber and Faber.

Gennard, J., and M.D. Steuer (1971), 'The Industrial Relations of Foreign Owned Subsidiaries in the United Kingdom', *British Journal of Industrial Relations*, IX, 143–59.

Gennard, J., S. Dunn and M. Wright (1980), 'The Extent of Closed Shop Arrangements in British Industry', *Employment Gazette*, LXXXVIII, 16–22.

George, K.D., R. McNabb and J. Shorey (1977), 'The Size of the Work

Unit and Labour Market Behaviour', *British Journal of Industrial Relations*, XV, 265–78.

Goodman, J.F.B., and J. Krislov (1974), 'Conciliation in Industrial Disputes in Great Britain: A Survey of the Attitudes of the Parties', *British Journal of Industrial Relations*, XII, 327–51.

Government Social Survey (1968), *Workplace Industrial Relations*, London: HMSO.

Grant, W., and D. Marsh (1977), *The CBI* , London: Hodder and Stoughton.

Hannah, L., and J.A. Kay (1977), *Concentration in Modern Industry*, London: Macmillan.

Hickson, D., and G. Mallory (1980), 'Scope for Choice in Strategic Decision Making and the Trade Union Role', paper presented to the Foundation for Management Education Conference, Henley-on-Thames (duplicated).

Hyman, R. (1972), *Strikes*, London: Fontana.

Lloyd, P.A. (1976), *Incentive Payment Systems*, London: British Institute of Management.

McCarthy, W.E.J. (1964), *The Closed Shop in Britain*, Oxford: Basil Blackwell.

McCarthy, W.E.J. (1966), *The Role of Shop Stewards in British Industrial Relations: A Survey of Existing Information and Research*, Donovan Commission Research Paper 1, London: HMSO.

McCarthy, W.E.J. (1967), *A Survey of Employers' Association Officials*, Donovan Commission Research Paper 7, London: HMSO.

McCarthy, W.E.J., and S.R. Parker (1968), *Shop Stewards and Workshop Relations: The Results of a Study Undertaken by the Government Social Survey for the Royal Commission on Trade Unions and Employers' Associations*, Donovan Commission Research Paper 10, London: HMSO.

McCarthy, W.E.J., and N.D. Ellis (1973), *Management by Agreement: An Alternative to the Industrial Relations Act*, London: Hutchinson.

MacKay, D., D. Boddy, J. Brack, J.S. Diack and N. Jones (1971), *Labour Markets under Different Employment Conditions*, London: Allen & Unwin.

Marsh, A.I. (1971), 'The Staffing of Industrial Relations Management in the Engineering Industry', *Industrial Relations Journal*, II, No. 2, 14–23.

Marsh, A.I., E.O. Evans and P. Garcia (1971), *Workplace Industrial Relations in Engineering*, London: EEF and Kogan Page.

National Board for Prices and Incomes (1968), *Payment by Results Systems*, Report No. 65, Cmnd 3627, London: HMSO. (N.B.P.I.)

National Board for Prices and Incomes (1968), *Job Evaluation*, Report No. 83, Cmnd 3772, London: HMSO.

Nie, N.H., C.H. Hull, J.G. Jenkins, K. Steinbrenner and D.H. Bent (1975), *Statistical Package for the Social Sciences*, 2nd edn, New York: McGraw-Hill.

Parker, S. (1974), *Workplace Industrial Relations 1972*, London: HMSO.

Parker, S. (1975), *Workplace Industrial Relations, 1973*, London: HMSO.

Paterson, T.T. (1956), 'Scale Factors in Coal Mining Labour Indices', *Operational Research Quarterly*, VII, 155–64.

Pay Board (1974), *Problems of Pay Relativities*, Advisory Report 2, Cmnd 5535, London: HMSO.

Pencavel, J.H. (1970), 'An Investigation into Industrial Strike Activity in Britain', *Economica*, XXXVII, 239–56.

Prais, S.J. (1976), *The Evolution of Giant Firms in Britain*, Cambridge: Cambridge University Press.

Price, R., and G.S. Bain (1976), 'Union Growth Revisited: 1948–1974 in Perspective', *British Journal of Industrial Relations*, XIV, 339–55.

Rees, A., and G.P. Shulz (1970), *Workers and Wages in an Urban Labor Market*, Chicago: University of Chicago Press.

Royal Commission on Trade Unions and Employers' Associations 1965–1968 (1968), *Report*, Cmnd 3623, London: HMSO.

Royal Commission on Trade Unions and Employers' Associations (1968), *Selected Written Evidence Submitted to the Royal Commission: Confederation of British Industry, the Trades Union Congress and Others*, London: HMSO.

Shalev, M. (1978), 'Lies, Damned Lies and Strike Statistics: The Measurement of Trends in Industrial Conflict', *The Resurgence of Class Conflict in Western Europe Since 1968*, vol. 1, ed. C. Crouch and A. Pizzorno, London: Macmillan, 1–19.

Shalev, M. (1978), 'Appendix II: Problems and Strike Measurement', *The Resurgence of Class Conflict in Western Europe Since 1968*, vol. 1, ed. C. Crouch and A. Pizzorno, London: Macmillan, 321–34.

Smith, C.T.B., R. Clifton, P. Makeham, S.W. Creigh and R.V. Burn (1978), *Strikes in Britain*, DE Manpower Paper No. 15, London: HMSO.

Stigler, G.J. (1962), 'Information in the Labor Market', *Journal of Political Economy*, LXX, Supplement to no. 5, S94–S105.

Thakur, M., and D. Gill (1976), *Job Evaluation in Practice*, London: Institute of Personnel Management.

Thomas, B., and D. Deaton (1977), *Labour Shortage and Economic Analysis*, Oxford: Basil Blackwell.

Thomson, A.W.J., and V.V. Murray (1976), *Grievance Procedures*, London: Saxon House.

Thomson, A.W.J., C. Mulvey and M. Farbman (1977), 'Bargaining Structure and Relative Earnings in Great Britain', *British Journal of Industrial Relations*, XV, 176–91.

Turner, H.A. (1969), *Is Britain Really Strike-Prone? A Review of the Incidence, Character and Costs of Industrial Conflict*, London: Cambridge University Press.

Turner H.A., G. Clack and G. Roberts (1967), *Labour Relations in the Motor Industry: A Study of Industrial Unrest and an International Comparison*, London: Allen & Unwin.

Weekes, B., M. Mellish, L. Dickens and J. Lloyd (1975), *Industrial Relations and the Limits of Law*, Oxford: Basil Blackwell.

Woodward, J. (1965), *Industrial Organization: Theory and Practice*, London: Oxford University Press.

Index of Secondary Authorities Cited

General Index